Praise for Sue Wieger

"Sue Wieger has a unique approach to golf and life that will help you unlock your true potential. By reading her book , GOLF - The Last Six Inches: Change your Brain, Change your Game, she will simplify your swing thoughts. More importantly she will harness and redirect your mind."

~Dr. Bobbi Lancaster, LPGA Tour Golfer

"With Sue's Change Your Brain, Change Your Game mental coaching strategies, I won my first professional tournament. Working with Sue has helped me change my focus and given me the tools for my success.

~Justin Spray, PGA Tour Professional

"Working with Sue and her Change Your Brain, Change Your Game tools, has been priceless to both my golf game and my personal life."

~Caroline Johnston, Gold Canyon, AZ

"It was so much more that what I anticipated the workshop to be, I learned how to lower my golf score and conquer my inner demons."

~Kristin Herffern, Breast Cancer Corporate Executive

"Sue's coaching is perfect for someone like me who gets so analytical with their game. I had self talk of shanking the ball and Sue's coaching taught me how to talk my way into great shots and results were immediate. It works and it's so easy and so relaxing."

~Karen Peterson, Club Champion, Payson AZ

"Sue's *Change Your Brain, Change Your Game* workshop

gave me so many golf and life lessons and it certainly has changed my game and my life."

~Cynthia, new golfer from Michigan

"In case you were wondering if I was paying attention, Sue... I just played my career best round of golf today." *(One day after taking the Change your Brain, Change your game retreat)*

~Nina Payson, AZ

"Sue's all about the "brain game!" I I've learned that my mind is a powerful tool and that positive thoughts produce excellent swings. I'm loving it! I'm so happy that Sue has put her wisdom into book form and made it accessible to a wider audience. I'm confident that GOLF: THE LAST SIX INCHES will move many more golfers to change their brains and change their games."

~Steve Holm, 6 Handicap

"I am grateful to have spent time with Sue Wieger and I am glad to be able to call her a good friend. Her knowledge in golf and her passion to help people is infectious. I am excited knowing that so many golfers will read her book and create profound new outcomes on the course."

~Bryan Hepler, Founder of Tathata Golf

GOLF

The Last Six Inches:

Change Your Brain, Change Your Game

By Sue Wieger M.Ed LPGA

GOLF - The Last Six Inches

Wieger Consulting, LLC
54 W. Pecan Place
Tempe, AZ 85284 USA

Phone: (480) 392-6563
Email: swieger@gmail.com
www.suewiegergolf.com

Ordering Information

Special discounts are available on quantity purchases by corporations, associations, and other organizations. For details, contact the publisher at the address above.

ISBN: 978-0-9968687-0-9

Printed in the United States of America

I dedicate this book to my lovely wife, Sheila, for her unconditional love and support.

I also dedicate this book to my golf clients, LPGA and PGA colleagues who inspire me to keep growing as a coach and as a person. Forever grateful for their continued support of Sue Wieger Golf.

Table of Contents

PREFACE

Let me first congratulate and thank you for purchasing *Golf - The Last Six Inches*. I am excited for you and the improvements you're about to make to your golf game and possibly your life. I'm positive if you work through this book, you will clearly see why your golf game, forgive the pun, has not been up to your par.

For those of you who may have had more traditional golf instruction in your past or might be just beginning golf instruction in your near future, I am wishing you an open heart and mind. This book will challenge you to think a little deeper about your golf improvement techniques and instruction. This book will teach you to think about your mindset first. In learning any new skill, including learning golf, your mindset needs to be present and actively engaged in the learning process This book, *Golf - The Last Six Inches*, will challenge your critical thinking skills, and give you some basic brain science knowledge on how your minds affects your golf game.

I quote Michael Hebron, PGA Master Professional and lifelong learner, "Mindset before Skill set".

You have taken the first step toward creating peak performance mindset on the golf course by opening this book.

This book is not just a golf instructional manual, but just might be a self help book as well. As you answer questions, and complete fun and engaging mental exercises in the book and *ACE Performance Training Guide*, some fears and vulnerabilities might arise. Do not fear those vulnerabilities for they are opportunities for the most potential growth to occur. Challenge those vulnerabilities and become aware of them so you can conquer them with tools learned in this book.

This book will help you address those vulnerabilities and create a shift by giving you tools to empower yourself on and off the golf course. Your mindset is the key to that shift. In these pages you will learn tools to elevate your game by creating a peak performance mindset.

I have used these tools for years and have seen drastic improvement in the way my students are thinking, and feeling about themselves. Their relationship with themselves has changed on the golf course. Players are golfing with no fear, and playing with more joy and happiness no matter the score outcome.

This book along with the *ACE Performance Training Guide*, which I feel is a must tool to have in order to dive deep into elevating your golf game You can talk about changing your golf game all day long and you can have thoughts about that change, but you really must do something about changing it. Meaning you must decide to take a different route and take action. This book and *The ACE Performance Training Guide* will give you the tools and strategies to creating a peak performance mindset.

Traditional golf instruction has been focused on mechanics, such as changing your grip, changing your stance, or changing your downswing. This book will not give you mechanical tips on your golf swing; however, it will give you the mechanics of creating a peak performance mindset.

When it comes to golf instruction, people often think there is nothing new to be learned. For the most part, that is true. The mechanics of the golf swing has been studied for years and with all the new technology we have today, golf instruction is getting tremendously over analytical in nature. This book is not about mechanics of a golf swing. This book is about how we think and feel about ourselves when we are on the golf course, which in turn drives our performance.

I have always wondered why golfers, who seem to have the same outstanding golfing skill sets, perform at different levels. What is the common link between the golfers that win and those golfers that don't? On both PGA and LPGA tours, players all have great golf swings, even though they may look different. What separates the peak performers from the participants? I believe it's their **mindset**. They all have exceptional mechanical skills. Think about it. Within both the LPGA and PGA touring professionals, they all have the skills to compete at the highest level. The question is why does the person with the most fundamentally sound golf swing not win tournaments or sustain peak performance? Why do amateurs play well one day and shoot their career worst the next day?

Golf - The Last Six Inches is written to help you answer some tough thought provoking questions such as: What is my mindset on and off the golf course? What would I like my mindset to be? Is there a new process in the way I think about my golf game? The answers you are searching for can be found here and in the companion workbook, *The ACE Performance Training Guide.* If you take the training guided activities and tools seriously and decide to actively engage in the exercises, your commitment will be rewarded with a peak performance mindset, golf game enhancement, and a joyful self- discovery process.

The *ACE Performance Training Guide* is full of questions, and exercises, and activities to challenge your thoughts and feelings. These critical thinking questions will open your eyes to your inner demons, and possibly some vulnerability you may have never addressed before now. I encourage you immediately go to this link https://golf-thelastsixinches.com and purchase The *ACE Performance Training Guide* for the guide is the necessary tool for your breakthrough

This book is to help you alter your way of thinking and feeling about how you approach your golf game and your life. I encourage you to take your time read each chapter and complete each chapter exercise found in *The ACE Performance Training Guide.* Take your time with each chapter's mental training activities and exercises so you do not rush through it. The book, and the *ACE Performance Training Guide,* is designed together so that you will gain insight about yourself and your golf game. Awareness is the first step of change and you have made that first step by purchasing the book.

These questions, activities, exercises, and thought processes will create feelings of possible vulnerability and potentially an attitude of fear of the unknown. Learning occurs when we step into that "unknown space", even when we don't succeed. Transforming the way you think around the golf course should be a challenge for you because it is a different approach that you probably never tried, or even knew how to do.

I suggest you read each chapter, and commit to completing the training exercises *in the ACE Performance Training Guide* so that you anchor in your new mindset learning. Remember change doesn't happen overnight, so decide and commit to the process you are about to begin.

When you take on a new goal, you set out with a plan or a strategy. At times that plan needs to be modified and that is permissible. Don't beat yourself up if your plan is to go through this book and the journal and you get side tracked or frustrated on one section. Take your time and enjoy the process. Play with one chapter at a time and one exercise at time. You may find one exercise may take you longer to learn and absorb than others. The stop and start over process is natural. Remember Rome wasn't built in a day and change doesn't work that way either. It is very important to be patient and be kind to yourself during this process of self- discovery and mental growth.

This book is not a quick fix. For your thoughts, feelings, and actions have been driving your golfing successes and failures to this point. Most golfers are looking for quick fixes in their golf games or swings. Be brave while reading this book, for you are stepping outside of your comfort zone to begin new way of thinking to achieve your golfing goals and growth. *Golf - The Last Six Inches* is meant to help you learn tools and strategies to create a shift in your thinking. By learning and applying these tools you will build a peak performance mindset and gain sustainability in the level of performance you desire.

Trust in yourself. Jump off that cliff of uncertainty. I know you will find powerful wings to fly on within this book.

Enjoy your journey of *Changing your Brain to Change your Game.*

YOUR NEXT STEP >>>>> Go to this link

https://golf-thelastsixinches.com

and get your ACE Performance Training Guide

INTRODUCTION

It was a beautiful summer day in Omaha, Nebraska; it was one of those top ten days on the golf course. The sun was shining, there was low humidity, and no wind. The temperature was pretty mild for a June day in Omaha.

I was playing in my first Women's City Amateur Championship at Elmwood Park Golf Course. I had just shot my best round of my three year golfing career of 69. Yes, a score 69 on par 72 public golf course. It was my first time ever breaking par. My final round of 69 was so easy. The golf swing felt great, and I was just playing in the zone. At that time early in my career, I didn't know what the zone was; I was such a young player. I was in my late 20s back then and had just picked up the game. I was a competitive three sport athlete in high school and college, but didn't pick up the game of golf until I was a senior in college. I picked up the game literally by accident securing a summer job at a golf course as a beer cart girl (now we call them food and beverage drivers). I watched players play the game on the golf course and decided to try the game myself thinking it didn't look that hard. My mentality was simple in theory: *"You just hit a ball from point A to point B, right?"* I had a beginner's childlike mindset back then.

I was pretty skillful in the beginning. I could hit the golf ball fairly far for a beginning player and fairly accurately. I know my early athletic skill development in tennis and softball helped out with understanding this new rotational game called golf. I fell in love with the game and played every chance I could. In Omaha, I joined a 9 hole ladies league to play every week and worked on my game after working my shift at the golf course. I was self-taught and just went out and learned how to play by playing all the time. Again, I just had the beginner's mind set. My thoughts were very simplistic; all I thought was, *"There is a target, so just hit it there."* My early amateur career came fairly easy, and my game improved every summer. The first time I kept score counting every shot, I shot 84 for 18 holes. I thought to myself, *"Well, that is not very good. It's not par, and I should be shooting par."* I really didn't know any better. My golf game got better and better, so I decided to start playing tournaments.

Back to the 69. I just shot myself into a championship playoff. I remembered swinging on the 18th hole on my last hole of regulation play, and I just thought, *"Wow, this is so easy today."* I was swinging with no thoughts, I could see my targets very clearly, and the ball went exactly where I wanted it to go. After posting my 69, I found out I was in a playoff with another good player I knew. She was a very consistent player; however, not a good as me (in my mind anyway). I could out drive her easily, giving me the advantage on the playoff hole.

We started the playoff after all participants finished the regulations rounds. When I found out I had made the playoff, I immediately started to think, *"Oh, I got this, I played so well today. This will be a piece of cake."*

Well, things changed as we got closer to the playoff. As time went on, I started to second guess myself and had thoughts of, "What if..." The "What Ifs" were not positive thoughts, they were negative. Thoughts like...

"Wow, this is my first playoff ever. What if I don't play well?"

"The other player is better than me, so I better play well."

"What if I don't out drive her on the first hole, then what?"

"What will people think of me if I lose this playoff after shooting a 69 today?"

My state of mind was definitely not the same as the mindset I had when I was shooting the earlier round of 69.

I got to the playoff hole tee box, and I was a totally different person. I was nervous and full of anxiety. The pressure was building, and it was definitely a different feeling than what I'd had when I played my final regulation round so easily.

My heart was racing; I was physically shaking. My thoughts were all over the board and not on my golf. We went to the tee box, and people started to gather around us to watch the playoff. It was so nerve-wracking having people actually watch me play. I was so worried about what other people were thinking about me at the time. I teed off and didn't even feel the shot; I was so nervous. I was giving all my focus and attention to everyone else and not the target or my game. I had close friends there that I played with before, but never in this pressure situation. My best friend at the time offered me a beer just to help me calm down because she knew I was very nervous. This was the first time in golf that I felt the pressure and let the pressure get to me. I played various collegiate athletics (basketball, softball, volleyball, and tennis), and I had been in many competitive situations. I had never felt that type of pressure. I have had many opportunities and situations in my athletic career to win games, such as making a free throw to win the game or serving an ace to win the state tennis titles match in high school. I have had those pressure situations and never felt like I did in this golf playoff. Each shot was crucial, and I felt like each shot was life or death. I was putting too much pressure on myself.

I approached my approach shot after hitting a great drive almost to the green on a par four. The shot ended up only 15 yards from the green. It was a simple wedge shot only 15 yards off the green. I had executed this shot many times before, but I missed and the ball went three feet in front of me. I was so embarrassed. I went up to the ball again, did the exact same thing, and chunked it again. I felt so humiliated and dejected.

The other player hit her shot onto the green from 80 yards away, and her shot landed in the center of the green. All I had to do was hit my shot close to secure a birdie putt. I approached my shot with a wedge and felt myself thinking many different thoughts...

"People are watching, you better hit this close."
"Now don't leave this short."

I basically gave up and hit a shot six inches from the hole. I went up and marked the ball. My opponent proceeded to two putt for par and won the play off. I was devastated. I knew I was the better player, so what the heck happened here?

I couldn't believe it. How could everything go so wrong when I had just shot a 69 earlier? Hours ago, everything was effortless and easy. Why the meltdown?

My skills in the playoff were not the same as earlier in the day. I was determined to find out why. After reflecting, I realized my **mindset** was the difference. It was the six inches between my ears that was the difference. My thoughts were not on the target, they were not positive, and I didn't have the belief system in place like earlier in the day. Earlier, I could not miss.

After much reflection, I knew in my heart that I could play this game competitively and at a high level. I knew in my heart that I had the skills to take my life on a new trajectory. I knew I had the skill sets even though I was still learning the game. This was my turning point. The last piece of my game that I needed was the mental piece. The last training I needed to do was focused on the six inches between my ears.

After six years playing amateur golf in Nebraska, I decided to turn professional. I had just turned 30 and had been teaching and coaching high school basketball. I wanted to see how far my game would take me. I knew I wanted to leave Nebraska to find a sunny place where I could play 12 months a year, so I started looking and sending hundreds of resumes to golf courses and resorts trying to secure a job in the golf industry. I had a Bachelor's in Education and thought that would help. I sent letters to golf courses and resorts all over Florida and Arizona, thinking these would be my best places to land a job. I could not get an interview anywhere, until one day a Director of Golf from Charlotte NC called me. I was excited just to have an interview. I ended up getting a job offer; however, the job started in April, only one month before my high school teaching contract was up. I decided to leave my teaching position, even though it was a No-No in education to leave a position before your contract was up. People were telling me, "What are you thinking? You are too old to play professional golf!" My passion for playing the game, learning the game, and working in the golf industry was driving my decision to leave my family, my home state, and my secure teaching career. I ended up leaving Nebraska to start my professional career. I just knew that this was my new journey.

When I arrived in Charlotte, I thought, *"Great, now that I am here, I can really get some great professional advice on my game and new career."* I began to entrust my game to the real professionals. I thought I should listen to all my new professional colleagues because they knew so much more than me. This is when I started to take lessons from every so-called professional that was willing to help me. In the business, most golf professionals don't charge each other for lessons. I wanted to be a sponge and learn as much as I could to get my game even better. That was my first mistake.

I started taking lessons from many different pros, and believe me, they all had their own method and way of swinging the golf club. I took every swing tip and tried every training aid

I could from my fellow professionals at the club to get better. I changed my swing and my equipment. I changed everything. I listened to every Tom, Dick, and Harry golf professional. I got worse. You know how it goes when you follow other people's advice instead of your own intuition? The result is that you get lost. I lost my swing, my confidence, and any trust I had in my ability to swing the club; you name it, I lost it.

Early in my career, I was getting worse, not better when turning professional. During this time, I was trying to play in professional golf tournaments in North Carolina, South Carolina, and Florida and gain my PGA card. This was summer of 1992, and back then, I was one of a few woman trying to get into the PGA to play professionally. You first have to pass the PGA Players Ability Test, which is a 36 hole tournament, and shoot a target score of 144 from 6900-7100 yardages. There were only six women I knew who could even compete at that level back in the early 90s. Even the LPGA tour players did not have to play from those long yardages. To say the least, I was playing horribly while listening to everyone share how to swing and how to play. I had many different methods being shown to me to help me get better; however, that was not the result I was getting.

The first Players Ability Test was in Hilton Head Country Club. I was the only woman in the field. I went to the golf club feeling nervous and had no idea what to expect since it was my first attempt. I walked into the golf shop and went to the shop counter. The professional at the counter said, "I am sorry, we don't have any tee times available, we have a PGA Players Ability Test going on here today." I said, "Yes, I know, I am one of your participants in the field." He asked for my name. I thought, *"Oh wow, here we go, they don't even know I exist."* My mind was racing and having all kinds of negative self-sabotaging thoughts. My palms were sweating, and my stomach was in knots and upset. I was actually feeling nauseous and felt like I was getting sick. I had not even hit a golf shot yet, but I was a wreck.

I went to the practice facility to hit some balls to try and calm down. I started to warm up and was hitting horrible shots. I was actually hitting shanks, and every golfer knows that that is the worst feeling shot in the world. Hitting shanks makes you even more fearful because it is the last shot you want to see before you go play.

I could not feel my hands or my swing. I was hitting shots, fats, thins, shots to the right, and shots to the left. I had absolutely no confidence and was scared to death.

My internal self-talk was incredibly negative...

"Sue, what have you done here? You moved away from family, are starting a new career, and you can't even hit a straight shot. What were you thinking?"

"The men here are looking at me, and I am sure they are thinking, 'What is the heck is she doing here? She can't play; she is shanking the ball.'"

The men participants were not very friendly and very absorbed into their own game and practice. They were all so serious. I would try and say hi to them to break the ice, but they were totally focused on practicing for their round. Another lesson I learned: men want to play, they don't want to socialize.

It was like I was their competitor, and they wanted nothing to do with me. My attitude was that the PAT was about shooting a target score and beating the golf course, not beating each other. However, these golf professionals were serious and anti-social. They treated me like a competitor, not a fellow golf professional. The support there was minimal, and the environment was very tense. This didn't help me at all. It made me feel worse.

After warming up, I walked over to the first tee to meet my fellow participants. We exchanged names, let each other know what type of ball we were playing, and exchanged scorecards. After that, we went to tee off.

I watched two players tee off, and then it was my turn. There was no wind and the humidity was high that day on the golf course. This was my first official professional tournament. I was so nervous; I can actually remember to this day the feeling I had on the tee box.

My legs were shaking so much that I don't remember hitting the golf ball. I hit my drive, and I actually felt like I whiffed the ball because I felt nothing. I looked down and the ball was gone. I asked my fellow players where my tee shot went, and they said, "Right down the middle." Too bad I didn't see it because that might have given me some confidence.

That first PAT was an eye opener for me. I was trying to do things I knew in my heart and soul I was not ready to do. I was playing from yardage of 7000 yards and there were par 5's. I had to try and hit my driver off the tee and then hit my driver off the fairway just to give myself a chance at getting the ball down far enough so I could have a long wood or long iron into the green in regulation. This was a different experience playing from those long yardages. This was not fun, and I remember trying very hard to hit shots I had no business trying to pull off. My score showed it.

Consequently, I didn't meet the target score, and I was disappointed again. My brain was focusing on all the different swing techniques my fellow pros were telling me to do. I was wrapped up in mechanics while trying different methods to find the right formula. I was not the same player I was back in Nebraska where I just went out, played, and scored well. I was too in my head. My game and confidence were in the tank.

I could not break 80 and even played in a member Pro Am where I was the Pro and shot 90. I was so embarrassed. This was my first year as a professional, and I was too frustrated to even play with members.

I played in three more PGA PATs. During the second PAT, I was paired with a gentleman from Florida. It was his 13th attempt at trying to pass the PAT. I said to myself, *"Oh wow, if he is still here, what the heck am I doing here? This is going to take forever, and I am not sure this is what I signed up for. This journey is not the way I want to live this life."*

I stopped playing for a while and just started to reflect on WHY I got into this game in the first place. I started to think about beginning my golf teaching career, so I sought out the best in the business. David Leadbetter, Jim Flick, Mike Hebron, John Jacobs, etc., you name them, I went to study from them and their philosophies. As I started my research, I began to realize they all had their own methods even though ball flight laws were pretty consistent. There are certain laws of physics that make the ball go where it goes and there is much cause and effect in the golf swing. When I dove into the teaching side, I started to realize I did have many of the proper skills already. That is why I originally played so well as an amateur. A childlike and beginner's mind helped my early days on the golf course.

My career changed when I went to a PGA Teaching Summit and met Dr. DeDe Owens. She was like me, a female in the business, a great teacher, and person who loved helping people. I sat and talked to her about my struggles, and she said to me, "Sue, you already have the skills, you just need to trust and believe in yourself. You have a teaching degree and great experience, so go follow your own passions."

That day changed my life. Dr. Owens also told me about the LPGA Teaching and Club division of the LPGA tour. I was down on my game and thinking that I was too old to play on tour. Then she told me about the LPGA Teaching and Club division which trains teachers how to teach. I was all in and went back to Charlotte with a new vision about my own game and career. I also tracked down Dana Radar, LPGA teaching professional in Charlotte (now National President of the LPGA), who was the former assistant at Myers Park CC where I was working in Charlotte and who left to start her own teaching business.

I met with her and was so impressed I joined the LPGA Teaching and Club Professional division that year. I went back to playing and started to play well again. I stopped listening to others and started to listen to myself, my own thoughts, and my own intuition. I started to listen to the six inches between my own ears. You know the thing called your own mind which is filled with your own thoughts. Hence the title *Golf - The Last Six Inches*. Focusing on those last six inches was the key to my transformation.

I became mindful of my own theories of self-learning, just like I did when I started the game. I figured it out for myself. I started to become very aware of my thoughts and self-talk, and I changed the negative to the positive mindset I had when I played as an amateur. I started to utilize this philosophy, not only in my golf game, but in my teaching philosophies and methodologies.

I started to use language of trust, love, happiness, and joy when I would practice. I learned to trust my own skills again and really became aware of the thoughts in my head.

I changed my attitude and mental training, and I finally passed my PGA Players Ability Test after four attempts. My training and preparation was totally different before my fourth PAT.

Why? My mental approach was so much better because my NEW WHY was engaged and aligned with my passions. I learned how to focus better, and I became aware and mindful of my attitude and belief system about my own game.

I had had the wrong mindset and beliefs. I lost my way because I didn't trust myself through the early professional days. If I only had the mental training I do today back then, my career might have turned out differently, but I love teaching and truly believe that is where most of my gifts lie.

During my amateur career, I didn't know any better. I had a beginner's childlike mindset. That mindset is based on being open and curious. I was lucky and started the game with the right mindset. This mindset is about keeping things simple, learning as you go, trusting yourself, and believing in yourself. All these concepts are about the thoughts and beliefs located in the six inches between your ears.

YOUR NEXT STEP >>>>> Go to this link

https://golf-thelastsixinches.com

and get your ACE Performance Training Guide

CHAPTER 1

Your WHY of Golf?

"Knowing is not enough; we must apply.
Willing is not enough; we must do."

–Johann Wolfgang von Goethe

Golf is called a game for a reason. The word game is defined as a form of play or sport, especially a competitive one, played according to rules and decided by skill, strength, or luck. The word PLAY sticks out for me. PLAY is defined as the engagement in activity for enjoyment and recreation rather than for a serious or practical purpose.

Are you playing the game of golf or working at the game of golf? As children, we played games. We were playful, curious, and had thoughts of unlimited possibilities. Play is first; we play even before we walk or speak. We don't ever want to stop playing. We must enrich it, build it, nurture it, and by all means, celebrate PLAY as many ways as possible!

So what happens? Life happens to us, and we create feelings and perceptions based on all those life events. Unfortunately, as adults, we lose that state of childlike curiosity as we experience life. We became tainted in the PLAY category. From conception to age seven, our brains are like a sponge; it is taking in everything from our surroundings, our culture, our parents, our exposure to light, darkness, everything. We don't have the ability to stop the incoming messages of people, places, and things around us. We are creatures in hypnosis, and our brain will capture all this stimulus and start to condition our habits and reactions to pain and love. Only after we turn six or seven, does our brain have the ability to problem solve and formulate our own decisions and really think and identify, *"No, stop. I don't want this."*

As adults, we close off our curiosity and feelings of newness. We also lose our ability to stay playful and open to experience. We shut down the "just wait and see" mentality. Our culture, educational setting, even our conditioning from family and friends create experiences of fear of failure, even fear of success. We tend to think, *"Well, but what if this happens or that happens?"* However, the "what if" thoughts are usually influenced by negative references, not the outcome of unlimited possibilities similar to the childlike state of being.

Golf is a game to be played. The game of golf is not a horrible and dreaded life threatening disease like cancer. Let's get real, and put this game into perspective. No one is putting a gun to your head to make you play this game. Golf is a game to be played, and this book will help you find ways to enrich your play and nurture yourself in this game.

MY FIRST WHY

When I first started playing golf, my WHY was that I was curious about the game that my brothers were playing. As explained in the introduction, my journey into golf was sort of an accident. It's amazing how one person or experience can change the trajectory of your life.

My first WHY was curiosity, but it soon turned into a more competitive WHY. I decided to get better and see how far I could take my game. I had a backup plan of teaching because I knew I could always fall back on teaching; so I jumped in with both feet and started my new journey as a golf professional.

As my touring professional experience was not making me happy (as explained in my story in the introduction), my love of teaching grew and my playing WHY began to change again. After realizing I just really wanted to teach golf, my soul and purpose was being fulfilled and my passion was growing to be the best teacher and coach possible. My WHY went from curiosity of the game to let's just see how far I could take my game and ended with the realization that I really just wanted to teach and help people learn and grow. I realized competitive golf was not my passion. My love of teaching was my motivation and WHY.

At the end of the chapter, you'll have an opportunity to write down your WHYs in *The ACE Performance Journal*. To help inspire you as you begin this process, I want to share with you the reasons WHY I PLAY.

MY CURRENT WHYS:

- I play for fun and enjoyment of the game itself. I often don't keep score in the game; however, I do keep an internal scorecard. (More about that later.)

- I play to see what type of great shots will come out of me each time I stand up over a ball. Golf gives me an opportunity full of unlimited possibilities and experiences. I truly love that variety.

- I love to play because I get to learn about myself every round I play. Adversity is a great challenge, and I love the various situations and playgrounds golf gives me.

- I build up my courage to play in a game that brings so much unknown. This game meets my needs of certainty, yet it gives me uncertainty.

- I love to play different courses because it gives me variety, not only in location but with the variety of shots to be played. In golf, we have different surroundings, different lies, and we can play from different tee boxes on the same golf course if we choose. Variety is what I enjoy about golf, and I love it. It is one of my most compelling WHY's. I am not the person who could play the same course over and over again.

- The certainty piece this game gives to me is that since I know that there is uncertainty out there on my next round of golf, I know that for certain there will be opportunities to learn about myself, learn from the environment, and learn from others which will challenge me. Self-learning is fascinating to me.

- I play to challenge my athletic skills and keep my body moving as I age. I love to play for the exercise.

- Golf is like an addiction. Golf gives me the ability to ground myself with nature. I love playing different golf courses around the world because it gives me so much pleasure feeling one with nature.

- Golf allows me to be with ME. It renders inner strength, courage, and inner peace. Yes, golf is an individual sport even though you play with many different people. Golf gives you a unique experience to learn so much about yourself.

- Golf is like a yoga mat; you just never know what your body will feel when you step onto the mat. The challenge is how you will respond to those feelings and experience. I get to be curious and open to all the possibilities meeting my internal drive for uncertainty.

- Golf allows you to just show up and go play with your inner child (if you let it be that way).

- I play because I love being outside in fresh air. I love the fresh smell of newly cut green grass.

- I absolutely love the sound of sprinklers going off on the fairway just before sunset.

- I love the feel of hitting the club's sweet spot on a driver. I love to play just to hear that sweet sound of the ball striking the center of the clubface. Simple, I know.

- I play because it challenges my inner being. Golf teaches me to discover more about myself every time I hit a golf shot. I learn something every time I play. It's a unique experience we are faced with in every round, every shot, and every putt. Golf will challenge your belief system. You never know what type of experience or golf shot you going to be faced with. It holds so true what Forrest Gump says, "Life like a box of chocolates, you just never know what you are going to get." So true in golf.

- I love to walk on the grass barefoot to feel grounded, and yes, I play barefoot sometimes.

- I love the feeling that I get to start over on every shot, every round. It gives me a sense of newness, and such a refreshing clean feeling.

- I love playing golf with fun, positive people.

- I love just to go play, not keep score. Just go play, no expectations. Just PLAY.

- I love to see what will come out of me on this next new round and how I deal with ME. It allows me to pay attention to my relationship with myself, and that is very empowering.

I hope you enjoyed reading my WHYs and found them inspiring. Remember, you'll have the opportunity to write down some of your WHYs in The *ACE Performance Journal*.

WHAT IS YOUR REAL ANSWER TO WHY
YOU PLAY THIS GAME?

Do you play for competition, challenge, exercise, social interaction, or does just being outside fulfill you? Do you play the game for yourself or for someone else? These are questions I often ask my clients and students. It seems many don't know the answers until they start to reflect on some deeper questions.

There is so much pressure to be someone we are not, nor want to become. For example, a golf instructor video tapes your golf swing and says, "Now let's compare your golf swing to Tiger Woods' swing." Come on, we are not all Tiger Woods. We are not built like Tiger Woods. We do not train or live like Annika Sorenstam.

Let's look at YOU! To be YOU in today's world. Hmmm...What a concept! Golf has the same challenges as life. For golf is a reflection of life. This book will show you how to THINK, FEEL, and PLAY by just BEING YOU. No one else, just your authentic, unique self. When we are ourselves, our unique gifts will show up.

It's important to understand your WHY. Why is it crucial to know your WHY? Your peak performance is wrapped up in your WHY. Your WHY can actually be the reason why you are not playing your best. Your WHY has to match your intentional actions and behaviors on the course. If you are playing this game for the wrong reasons, you will not find any joy or fulfillment in the game, and your performance will reflect this misalignment. The game of golf should not be taken so seriously, unless you are a PGA or LPGA tour player making a living at the game.

The reason I ask you to know your WHY is you will then start to consciously become aware of one of the most important factors in peak performance called motivation. If you are motivated by social golf, yet feel hampered by the anxiety of having to post a score every time you play, you are not aligned with your golf game WHY. This is the reason you don't show up as yourself when you play golf. You are too worried and distracted by all the other things going around you. If you are social golfer and you are put in a competitive situation, do you stay in the emotional state of a social golfer or do you turn into a competitive fighter, scratching for every inch on your driver length and swinging harder than you normally would that day?

There are some skilled players who want to play on the tour. These players' WHY is very different from an amateur who just wants to enjoy themselves and play social golf. Tour players have a different compelling reason to play this game. Do you see yourself on PGA or LPGA tour? That is a different WHY than someone else's.

There are other players who want to have fun, get better, be outside with friends, and socialize. Not any less a compelling WHY, just a different WHY. However, if this type of player tries to play and has expectations like the tour player, there will be a misalignment, and the experiences and outcomes will not be positive. There will be no joy or happiness in that experience of golf.

Your WHYs will make or break your peak performance state on the golf course. Without an empowering WHY, how can you grow as a player and human being? Without a compelling or empowering WHY, how can you move forward to further learning and achievement? Are you being honest with yourself about WHY you play? Be truthful to yourself about WHY you play.

Without a powerful WHY, your game will not evolve because your reasons are not compelling enough to pull or move you forward. Without powerful reasons, you lose your energy and motivation. Your WHY is your inspiration and your passion pill. You will want to thrive and take action to achieve more and get better if you are connected to your real WHYs. You will not need a boot camp trainer to push you like they do on *The Biggest Loser*. You have your own reasons, passions, and motivations. Your compelling WHY will always pull you forward if you stay engaged with it. If your WHY is compelling, your true passion for self-actualization as a person and player will shine through.

I have my clients make their list on a home play assignment in my lessons. I give them a journal to start making notes as they notice what their thoughts are about playing this game. Then they write down what comes to mind. They are somewhat amazed about what starts to come up for them because, for the first time, they are paying attention and noticing their actual thoughts. They start listening to their inner voice. Most obstacles we create are in our minds. Wouldn't it be nice to play golf with no obstacles? You'll have the opportunity to make these notes in your *ACE Performance Journal*.

Your mind can be free of obstacles as well if you let it be. Think about that statement. That inner voice gives you the correct directions if you are mindful of that voice. It is the same as a GPS system. The mind will know where to go if you just begin listen to it. If you listen to that inner voice within the last six inches between your ears, it has the correct yardage, club, feeling, instinct, and strategy for you to take. Your GPS system will guide you to your peak performance. I guarantee that if you listen and trust in your WHY, you really play this game, you will achieve different outcomes. Does this mean we can't take direction, hire a expert, or get advice or support from someone else? No, of course not. I feel you still need that type of feedback, but who you are and understanding your WHY are the critical elements to achieving a fulfilling golf game and a happy life.

HAVE COURAGE TO PLAY FOR YOUR OWN REASONS &
SET YOUR OWN BENCHMARKS.

Many times, players are not clear about their WHYs. I often hear this statement, "I am playing because my work colleagues play, and I feel like I have to keep up with them. My colleagues tell me I must play to get more business." Is it in your belief and story that the only way to obtain more clients is to play golf? Do you believe this to be true? Whatever you believe to be true will be true in your perspective. Do you enjoy getting new clients? Is it your belief that the only way to accomplish this is to play golf with your colleagues? I have clients who do not enjoy the game because they feel they are forced to play due to work. Do you have social or work pressure to play golf?

In my opinion, this is not the right WHY. You should enjoy what you do no matter what you do. If the WHY outcome is to build relationships with your clients and meet new people, then your WHY is different, and how you show up on the golf course will be different. I have clients that play for work pressure. If you are forced to play, then create a new WHY that is more uplifting. This will create a new experience and new memory of PLAY. You need to always enjoy yourself. If your WHY matches your actions, you will have a better outcome, experience, and better fulfillment.

When you create a positive WHY, it matches your motivation to play and it creates a PLAY state of mind not a trying state of mind. Positive WHYs give you the following:

- Positive WHYs build self-esteem and self-efficacy.

- Positive WHYs motivate you and pull you forward.

- Positive WHYs give you the fuel to follow through and stay engaged in your activity or goals.

- Positive WHYs create positive emotions that fill up your body with endorphins, which in turn creates feeling of happiness and joy. This happens when you are in love with something or someone.

What positive feelings do you get out of playing golf? Happiness, joy, fun, playfulness? If it doesn't give you joy or happiness, and it's giving you anxiety, fear, or doubt, just how long do you think you will keep playing a game that gives you such harsh feelings?

Humans have an innate ability called fight or flight response. It means we will either fight it or we will escape from the situation. For example, the largest demographic coming into the game is women; however, the fastest growing demographic leaving the game is women as well.

WHY? Too many times, a woman's first exposure to golf is not a positive one. The game starts off intimidating, and she gets thrown into competitive situations when she is not ready nor does she want to play competitively. Women want to play this game for different reasons than men. Many times, the game's culture is to be competitive and keep score. Women are social creatures. They like to network and feel a sense of belonging within their community. If they don't feel welcome, they don't stick around too long, hence, the case of women demographics leaving the game of golf. We need to change the culture to be an open, safe, and friendly environment so everyone will be welcome.

Think about when you first fell in love with someone. You felt like nothing could go wrong, and you were in PLAY mode with your first love. Nothing they did or said was taken negatively and everything was blissful. This honeymoon effect can, and will, happen in golf. However, as time passes, we start focusing on what's wrong with the person or the situation, and we start falling out of love. The focus changes and you lose the reason why you fell in love in the first place. It happens in every aspect of our lives if we don't stay connected to why we first loved this person or situation. Remember and focus on those reasons. In golf, remember WHY you are playing the game and your focus and performance will change. Create that "in love" feeling or state of mind when playing golf.

Each person's WHYs are different, and it is crucial to create a positive WHY so one can enjoy the experience. If you enjoy something, peak performance has a great chance of showing up.

When you connect to your WHY, you will always manage

yourself much better. You will nurture yourself just like the greens crew nurtures the golf course. They keep the fairways freshly manicured. Staying connected to your WHY will always keep you growing and thriving. You will also create harmony in your game and allow creative playgrounds to re-appear in your life. Your WHY will keep you fulfilled and playing for YOU, no one else.

The hardest thing in life is to be yourself and trust yourself under pressure or in situations that make you uncomfortable. Remember, you get to choose your WHY and your responses to life occurrences that challenge your reasoning.

Case study #1 - Why Play Golf?

Two company presidents start playing golf because they want to build a new client base and build relationships with their new and existing clients. President A took lessons and goes out and plays with his colleagues in a scramble event. He doesn't play well, but enjoys getting to know his clients. He begins to realize that golf is a great way to spend quality time away from the corporate boardroom meetings and build solid relationships with his clients.

President B takes a few lessons because he is self-conscious about his skill level and feels he must be a good golfer to impress his clients and fit in. He then plays in a scramble event with clients. He doesn't play well and is extremely nervous because he is worried about what his clients will think of his golf skill level. He fears they will compare it to his business savvy. He doesn't really like the game, but feels he needs to play to gain an edge on his working buddies.

Which player do you think will eventually leave the game or eventually start hating the game? Do you think the WHYs don't match with their inner beliefs as to the reasons why they are there in the first place?

They both originally said they wanted to build client relationships, but President A stays connected to his WHY while he is playing. He doesn't care about his score or his playing ability because his WHY is to build relationships. President B is anxious about his playing ability and loses his WHY. He says he wants to build relationship, but really he only wants to impress his clients. He doesn't enjoy the game or the time with his clients. How different is the scramble outcome and experience for these two company presidents? How do you think they will show up on the golf course? What type of actual golf performance experience will they have?

If golf is not the answer for you in the corporate world, then do not play. Please understand, I am not here to decrease new golf participants; however, this type of person will not stay engaged in the game anyway. Play for your own reasons.

Case study #2 - Couples & Golf

Another WHY I hear from my clients is, "Well, my wife or husband plays. If I want to see him/her, I need to learn how to play." Do you think this WHY will hold up very long once they start playing? Depending on the couple's relationship, this reasoning might be aligned with each other's WHY.

A woman wanted to begin to play golf because her husband played three to four times a week since retirement. Her WHY was to be with her husband and spend time with him. His WHY was to play golf to be competitive and challenge himself. When the couple started playing together, they didn't enjoy the experience. The husband would give swing tips on every swing and be critical with his wife. She didn't know all the rules of the game at times, didn't hit the ball as far as him, didn't know how to keep score, and didn't know where to drive the cart. After the woman came to me for her golf lesson, I realized they were playing for different reasons. I explained to her that we needed to have a couples lesson and explain the concept to them.

After our golf mental sessions, they both realized each other's reasons and motivations. They both wanted to play with each other, and they both started to understand each others WHYs. They made a decision going forward to only play golf with each other for the reason of just being together with no pressure to keep score or have swing lesson on the course; just to go play and enjoy each other's company. They made a pact with each other that their rounds of golf would be to socialize with each other and enjoy their free time together. The time would be spent for fun, no scoring or rules except common courtesy and etiquette. Now they play golf with each other every other week and love being together. The husband gets his other competitive challenging golf when he plays with the guys.

Another couple comes to me for joint lessons. The husband plays every week, and the wife is just starting to learn the game. The husband wants the wife to play with him, and the wife wants to play with her husband since he is spending more time on the golf course. The husband just wants her to learn the game and be able to play and have fun with him on social golf days. He is not interested in getting her into competitions or play dates with his buddies unless she desires.

With this couple, we go out on the golf course, and the husband is kind, loving, and patient with his wife's learning process. This couple enjoys their time together. They didn't keep score; they were just enjoying their time outside in a different environment than they have experienced before. They come back to the lesson tee with smiles on their faces, and they said, "Well, we played together and we didn't get a divorce. It was actually fun." They stayed connected to both their WHYS. Their intent was to play together and spend time participating in a different activity that both could enjoy. Their WHYs matched their outcome, and they just played for the simple reason of the enjoyment of being with each other.

A third couple comes to my lesson tee for joint lessons. The husband plays three times or more a week, and the wife is starting to pick up the game. The wife wants to play with her husband since he is spending so much time on the golf course.

This third couple took a couple swing lessons, and the husband also took his wife on the golf course by himself. They drove down middle of fairway with the husband driving the golf cart. The husband drove up to his golf ball on the fairway and asked the wife to drive the golf cart up to the green. The wife had never been on the golf course, let alone knew where to park the golf cart near or around the green. The wife proceeded to literally drive the golf cart onto the green like her husband asked her to do. The husband started screaming at her with language I can't even type in this book. This was an actual client of mine. They got in a huge argument.

After, the wife came back to the lesson tee alone and told me that story. She said to her husband, "I am never playing golf with you again." I was surprised she came back for more lessons after that horrible experience. She explained that she wanted to play the game on her terms, not his. They both decided to play separately because their WHYs were different. Great news; instead of trying to be someone they were not, they both decided to enjoy the game from different perspectives. Their WHYs were not aligned, so they didn't enjoy the time together on the golf course. They still love each other and accept each other for who they are. They both have a deeper respect for each other because they learned an important lesson with each other on the golf course. I hope one day they do decide to play together because they still love each other. Hopefully, that love will outweigh the competition he wants out of the game and the separation it is causing them.

Did this husband have the same WHY as his wife? Ultimately, I don't think so. If he did, he would have been more in tune with his wife's skill and knowledge level of the game. Did they want the same outcomes? They originally thought so, but came to realize their WHYs were really different. They became aware and accepted each other for who they both are in their core.

Many couples do not play with each other, which I think is sad. Alignment is as important as the why you are playing, and what you want to accomplish on the golf course for it will determine your outcome. If they are not aligned as to what the real reason is they are playing with each other, they will not enjoy the experience. If you start playing as a couple, it a great idea to discuss your WHYs and reasons you want to play with each other. You may find your reasons to be the same or maybe not the same. Be true to yourself no matter what happens and life will flow.

You should want to do what you want with your time. Finding common bonds or building relationships is a great outcome; however, it must match your wanted outcome. If it doesn't match, you will not receive the wanted outcome and you will end up with the opposite outcome like the last couple spending less time with each other. Let's hope they can find common aligned space on the golf course where they can be themselves and still enjoy each other.

I hear so many stories from my clients stating, "Oh I can't play with my spouse because they drive me crazy." We now know the reasons. They don't play for the same reasons, and it doesn't take a bad experience on the golf course or a yelling match on the course to find this out. Couples just need to really ask each other, "Why do you want to play with me?" If couples would address their WHY and be honest with each other, they would have stronger relationships with themselves and each other.

Couples would be so much happier on the golf course together because there would be understanding about each other's real intent, not some crazy unspoken expectation. Life is too short to not to enjoy what you do with your life and who you spend your time with.

Case study # 3 - A Competitive Women Golfer (HDCP 14)

A country club member came to my lesson tee wanting to be competitive in her country club championships. It seemed in her past competitive experiences, her anxiety and stress levels would be very high weeks before the competitions. She would get all worked up and tied up in knots so much so that her stomach would hurt and be upset days before the competition. Day of the competition, she would be physically sick from the anxiety build up. At times, she would play well, then have blow up holes and the snowball of negative self-talk took over. She would walk off the golf course in tears and anchor those experiences of frustration, anger, embarrassment and disappointment.

When she came to me, our first session was about her WHYs. We talked about WHY she was playing golf, and she made her list. Her list had nothing about winning the club championship. The list was full of items such as:

I love the game.
I love the challenge it gives me.
I love playing golf with my friends and enjoy
them tremendously.

She was playing golf for social reasons, but trying to put herself in a competitive state which she had no business trying to be in. Her anxiety rose as a result of her WHY misalignment. After a few sessions with me, we worked on some PSYCH-K whole brain balancing and reframing her WHY. PSYCH-K is a program designed to rewire your belief systems using muscle testing. We talked about her belief systems getting in the way of her showing up as her true self. Her true self is a loving, giving, funny, and compassionate human being. She realized she was not giving herself any self-love. Everyone was trying to give her love, but she was not accepting it because she didn't believe she deserved it. Utilizing my PSYCH-K facilitations, she began to own who she really was, and her WHY and belief system started to align.

Her mindset started to change when she played golf. She had less anxiety or fear of "what ifs" and no longer worried about the future. She started enjoying who she played with and why she played golf. Weeks before the tournaments, she stopped worrying about the future because it was not here yet. I taught her to live in the present and be grateful for each day. Once she learned that she could not control the future and could not change the past, she started enjoying herself. Stay in the present for the future isn't here yet, and the past is already gone. You can't control either of them.

She started to show up differently on the golf course. She played in her country club championship, and for the first time in years, she enjoyed her round of golf and played wonderfully. Her experiences were not her past history of blow up holes or anxiety ridden experiences. How did she accomplish this? She stayed connected to her WHY the whole round. The week before the tourney, she did not feel anxious; she was looking forward to playing in the championship. Her intent was to play with love in her heart, enjoy who she was playing with, and learn more about herself on the golf course. She stayed engaged in her WHY and her experience was transformational. Her golf game skill level also improved and we didn't even touch her golf swing. She actually won her flight and embraced her new found energy of loving herself. She went from a 14 handicap to a solid eight.

It took her a few competitive rounds to be fully engaged and totally focused on her WHY. We rewired her subconscious with PSYCH-K work. Results were outstanding, and now she is playing with love in her heart and playing extremely well in competition. Now she shows up not in an anxiety ridden state, but with love for the game and full of self-love. Her performance is enhanced which further reinforces her true self state. She now has a totally different experience when playing in competition because she stays engaged in her WHY, her intent, and her purpose. You will have real results when you match your WHY to your true self.

If you are someone who keeps score, that is okay. Keeping score can help us with reflective appraisals of skill and self-awareness. It allows an opportunity for intentional learning. If keeping score empowers you, then keep score. If keeping score disempowers you, then don't keep score. Is scoring a measurement tool for you? If so, in what way? Maybe it is just an awareness and growth tool to assess where you are in the game and where you want to be. What does keeping score really mean for you? Reflect back on why you play and why you keep score.

As a LPGA Professional, I keep score when I play in Pro Ams or competitions only. I don't want the score to dictate my experience ever. I love playing the game just to play because that's empowering for me. The score itself doesn't empower me. Don't keep it if it is not empowering.

If you are staying true to your intent, you will enjoy the game more. When you enjoy the game, your performance changes because you are aligned with your true essence and you don't have to fight your belief systems. Your subconscious will stay in tune with who you want to be.

THE WHY NOTS ON THE GOLF COURSE

If you play golf for the wrong reasons, think about how you will play. Will the round be a fun successful round, or will the round be long and unsuccessful? If your mind and thoughts are conflicting with the belief of why you are there, you can count on a not-so-nice round of golf, and you will not enjoy your time on the golf course.

Most people play golf to be social with other people. However, at times, we see people on the golf course who are angry, throwing clubs, and using foul language, etc. These people tend to be internally frustrated. Many times, they end up projecting their frustration with unhealthy social behaviors, such as being rude or even being mean to other golfers on the golf course. They tend to try and intimidate people by their unkind actions such as walking through people's lines of putt or talking in your backswing. These people try to sabotage your game by saying things like, "Wow, you are not playing very well today," or "I hope you don't three putts like you did the last hole."

These people need to put other people down to build themselves up and to make themselves feel better. Unfortunately, personal insecurity drives their unkind actions and behaviors. These people are not aligned with their WHY, and they play the game for self-esteem building. I don't believe people maliciously or consciously walk through other people's lines to make themselves feel better. However, they do subconsciously because this world is full of people needing to put other people down so they feel better.

Do yourself a favor and keep being true to yourself and who you are, and the next time someone is irritating, you won't feel the need to give it any energy. Golf is like water off a duck's back. I don't want to play like that. When people cut you off on the freeway, you will learn to respond differently. What if you could deflect this unhealthy energy and stay in your personal power and allow that to guide you to peak performance? In golf, just like life, you want your mind to be like a new garden every day. You want it to be free of weeds, and freshly manicured. Treat your mind like a garden, manicure it, keep it clean, nurture it. What do you do to a garden when you want something to grow? You nurture it, trim it, cut it, fertilize, and create this beautiful new fresh plant or produce. If you don't nurture, the garden will die or weeds will invade and destroy it. I don't need to tell you what it will look or feel like. The same is true about the last six inches - your mind. Nurture it, challenge it by feeding it with nutrients of positive thoughts. Nurturing, feeding, and continually growing yourself will enhance your soul, your spirit, and your mind. This nurturing will guide you and pull you forward as an engaged human being.

GOAL SETTING

Setting goals in your golf game is a great strategy; however, those goals must match your WHY in order for success. If your goals are aligned with your WHY, the energy you spend on your game will be uplifting and rewarding. If your goals are not aligned with what you want, your WHY, failure is certain and growth will not happen. Your WHY will keep you engaged in your action game plan whether it's swing improvement or on course management improvements. If you lose your WHY, you lose your motivation, and failure is certain.

A great example of people losing their WHY are New Year's Resolutions. Every year, corporate gyms and fitness companies have promotions to join their gyms and fitness programs. What does everyone like to do at the beginning of the year? Lose weight or start a fitness regimen. People set New Year Resolutions with the intent to lose weight and gain some health and wellness.

Many people start programs in January because it's a new year. National gyms are experts at marketing for new year memberships to build revenue every year. People join, but many fail to first list their compelling reason WHY they chose to join the gym. The psychology of starting anew every year is a fabulous marketing strategy for gyms. It's human behavior to start fresh and create new goals every new year.

What if you started to ask yourself the important questions, such as why do I want to join this gym? What do I really want out of joining this gym? What's my real WHY? To feel sexy. To lose weight. To feel light and healthy every day. You want to have positive WHYs. Positive WHYs create an emotion that will pull you forward and help you stay connected to the reason you are making this decision to join the gym. People who lose motivation don't feel successful and plateau. Drop offs occur every year in gyms across the country.

Going to the gym evolves into the feeling of work, and people lose their reasons and the routine becomes not fun. The same result may happen in the game of golf. Know your WHY and you will personally gain more confidence and feel compelled to follow through. You will be much more engaged in the process.

In golf, you have to learn to discipline yourself to stay engaged shot by shot by staying connected to your WHY. If you accomplish that connection and focus on every shot, your experience, on and off the golf course, will be transformed. Understanding your true self will not only enhance your golf game, but will carry over into every aspect of your life. Your life will transform in front of you because you are aligned to who you really are. There will be no more trying to be someone you are not.

The key is to create your true self state and your peak performance will take care of itself. Don't let anyone or anything take your WHY away from you. You do have control of that. You don't have control of people, situations, weather, green speed, rough height, etc., but you do have control on how you respond to them. You are the only one that can allow external factors to affect you.

Chapter 1 - ACE Performance Training Guide Homework

Go to Chapter One **Your Why of Golf** in your guide and answer the reflective questions and complete the Extrinsic versus Intrinsic Reasons exercise.

If you haven't already purchased and downloaded your copy of ***The ACE Performance Training Guide,*** you can get it here:

https://golf-thelastsixinches.com

***

Congratulations, you just took the first step toward

empowering yourself and your golf game.
Knowing your WHY is powerful!

CHAPTER 2

How Thoughts, Emotions, & Actions Dictate Your Golf Shots

"Play your game your way."

– Billie Jean King

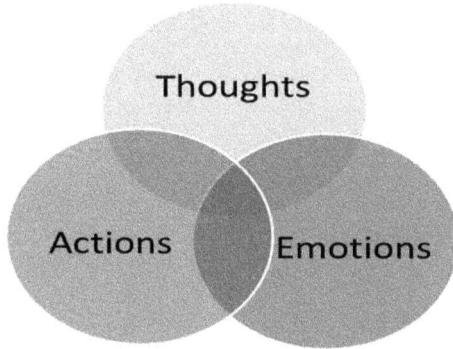

The top influence in your game is located within the six inches between your ears - your mind.

There is a direct correlation between your mind and your golf game. First, we will explain the relationship of thoughts, emotions, and actions in your golf game.

In the performance cycle, you have thoughts, then you have emotions, and then you have actions. Let's first focus on all of your thoughts and where they come from.

According to the National Science Foundation, we have over 50,000 thoughts running through our minds daily. Our conscious mind controls only 5% of our thoughts, and our subconscious mind runs 95% of our thoughts.

Our subconscious mind is the driver of our lives, on and off the golf course. Our self-image is buried within our subconscious.[1]

The conscious mind has the following distinctions:

- Sets goals and judges results.
- Thinks abstractly about new, creative ideas and activities.
- Is time bound, and past and future focused. The subconscious mind often looks for new ways to do things based on past experiences and future goals.
- Short term memory is stored here and that is only about 20 seconds in the average human being.
- Has limited processing capacity and only processes an average of 40 bits of information per second.
- Is capable of managing just a few tasks at a time.

The subconscious mind distinctions:

- Habitual: it monitors the operation of the body, including motor function (golf swing), heart rate, respiration and digestion.
- Thinks like a child. It knows the world through the five senses: hearing, seeing, feeling, tasting, and smelling.
- Long term memory is stored here. It stores past experiences, attitudes, values, and beliefs.

---

[1] Psych-K, by Rob Williams, M.A. (Psych-K, by Rob Williams, M.A.)

http://www.peace.ca/psych-k.htm

- The subconscious mind is timeless. It focuses on the present time only and uses past learning experiences to perform current functions, such as walking, talking, driving a car and so on.

What does your subconscious have to do with your golf swing? **EVERYTHING!**

If your subconscious mind knows you are a great putter, then yourself image is that of a great putter.

If your subconscious believes you are a lousy putter, then your self-image shows up as a lousy putter.

You can talk all day long to yourself and say, "I'm a great putter, I am a great putter," but if your belief system in your subconscious mind doesn't align with that comment, you are only fooling yourself. Then the real truth comes out and not so good putting strokes show up for you.

To change your thoughts, you must get to the subconscious level to rewire the nervous system. The new brain research tells us our brain is not a fixed machine, but actually an organ of neuroplasticity, which means it can change. We have new research coming out daily telling us the brain can change itself and change the function and structure to help transform our daily lives. In the book *The Brain That Changes Itself*, by Norman Doidge, M.D Dr. Doidge shares many stories about how the neuroplastic revolution has implications on many facets in our lives, not just the golf swing.[2]

To understand your performance cycle in your golf game, you must be first mindful of your thoughts.

Your thoughts will drive certain emotions, and those emotions will drive certain actions, such as your golf swing at that moment.

Let's go through the performance cycle of thoughts,

---

[2] Doidge, Norman. The Brain That Changes Itself: Stories of Personal Triumph from the Frontiers of Brain Science. New York: Viking, 2007.

emotions, and actions of a player who will be joining a new group of players on the golf course. This player does not know who they will be playing with until they get to the golf course. He realizes they have lower handicaps than him, and the handicaps are listed on their scorecard that is given at the beginning of the round card.

The player starts to have some thoughts that bring up some emotions, *"Well, they probably think I am a terrible player since my handicap is so high. My handicap is a 25 and their handicaps are all mid-teens. OMG, what am I doing here? I don't belong with this group! I knew I should not have come out to play today. It's not going to be a good day for me now."*

With these thoughts, what type of emotions do you think this player is having? Possibly some fear, insecurity, and anxiety. He is going to be very self-conscious on the tee. These types of emotions will generate other thoughts, *"They will be judging me all day. These guys are not going to like me and just might start rejecting me as a person."* All these thoughts, and the player hasn't even hit his first shot yet. This is how the cycle begins.

Where do thoughts go from here? Next thing that happens in the golf performance cycle of thoughts, emotions, and action is the body starts to react to these emotions. Our emotions will drive chemicals, called stress hormones, and the body will begin to react. Muscles begin tightening up, we start to feel tense, our body will even start to lose range of motion, which we all know is devastating to long drives off the tee box. Muscles will not work in unison with each other, so timing and rhythm will be affected. Golf is a dynamic motion, and many muscles must work together, yet separately, to perform efficient swings. Coordination will decrease. People with negative emotions firing through their body tend to breathe from their chest, and oxygen is then limited to major organs. The body will not produce the fluid golf swing. The person will then start to try to control a lot of their movements within their golf swings. Once the trying starts and the trust stops, motion is affected.

What type of golf shots do you think they're going to get from feeling this way?

Can you see how the process of your thoughts creates an emotion and those emotions create the physical action called your golf swing? How the body feels is what's generating the golf swing, so let's now focus on the emotions that come in with that golf cycle.

Some examples of empowering or positive emotions are feeling relaxed, happy, joy, trust, gratefulness, and feeling okay with being there since you can be yourself.

Now, let's look at the cycle of performance for the player thinking they are a terrible player. That thought will generate feelings of intimidation, fear, and anxiety. They're going to start trying. We have a lot of different chemical reactions in our body when we are stressed. What type of golf shots do you think will come out of that particular person if they're intimidated, anxious, and fearful? Have you ever felt that way before on a tee shot, on a putt or golf shot, or playing during a round? What kind of shots did you get from those type of thoughts and those type of emotions?

Your golf performance cycle starts from your thoughts, and the good news is you can control your thoughts. You can't control the weather, or the people you are playing with, but you can control your thoughts.

If you learn how to control your thoughts, you will learn how to create peak performances.

Anger

Aggressive, bitter, cold, competitive, defensive, disgusted, disrespected, enraged, frustrated, hostile, jealous, mad, outraged, pressured, resentful, revolted

Fear

Anxious, avoidant, cautious, concerned, fearful, frozen, insecure, intimidated, guarded, overwhelmed, panicked, stressed, tense, terrified, trapped, vulnerable, worried

Sadness

Apathetic, depressed, disheartened, disappointed, disillusioned, embarrassed, grief-stricken, guilty, hurt, lonely, needy, raw, regretful, rejected, shameful, stuck, tired, weak

Joy

Blissful, brave, confident, connected, ecstatic, energized, excited, friendly, happy, hopeful, loved, loving, proud, powerful, rebellious, relieved, relaxed, spiritual, strong, thankful, tough

The Complete Golf Cycle

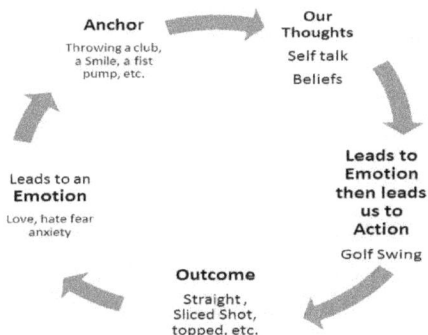

Anchor
Throwing a club,
a Smile, a fist
pump, etc.

Our Thoughts
Self talk
Beliefs

Leads to Emotion then leads us to Action
Golf Swing

Leads to an Emotion
Love, hate fear
anxiety

Outcome
Straight,
Sliced Shot,
topped, etc.

The Complete Golf Cycle includes thoughts, emotions, action, outcome, and anchors. Our thoughts come from our belief systems and self-talk buried in our subconscious. Those thoughts activate our emotions, and those emotions lead us to what's called an action, your golf swing, such as a straight shot, slice shot, top shot, hook shot, whatever that may be at that moment in time.

The outcome of the shot then will create another emotion which we either choose to anchor or neutralize. We will talk more about this anchoring system in the post shot routine section of the book.

After the shot, we're going to have emotion, and we are either going to like it, love it, or not like it. The word hate could be a strong word here, but you might feel that way...

When golfers hit bad shots, they tend to start thinking about what they did mechanically wrong. Many players will start breaking down their swing looking for answers to the last poor shot. Poor shots usually result in a negative thought such as frustration or anger. If golfers do not understand how to close that last poor shot and let it go, they anchor that emotion of frustration with the experience. They are now tied together in the nervous system and the mind will remember. Also, if players do not learn how to close the shot and let it go, they will hold onto the frustration and carry that negative emotion into their next shot.

Anchoring our emotions is a choice. We can either anchor the positive emotions or the negative emotions after shots. The important concept here is to be mindful of which emotions we are anchoring

Negative Anchors

- Physically throwing a club.
- Hitting a club against the ground violently.
- Screaming at yourself, "You are an idiot!".
- Walking off the golf course mad and upset about things you can't control.
- Walking down the fairway to your next shot like the world is coming to an end.
- Negative self-talk, such as beating yourself verbally in your external and internal language.

Positive Anchors

- Saying statements like, "Yes, that was more like me!"
- Fist pump to physically congratulate yourself.
- Squeeze the club after a good shot.
- Literally patting yourself on the back or shoulder after a good shot.
- Find something you can own the shot with either a verbal statement and anchor it with a physical cue. You can create your own.

The reason we want to use a physical cue is because it will increase your chances of anchoring the feeling of success and confidence within your nervous system. Remember, we want to anchor in the good shots and neutralize the bad shots.

Your brain and nervous system will anchor whatever emotion is tied to the golf shot. The good news is you can react or respond, but first you must be mindful of your patterns on how you currently anchor shots. Determining your pattern will help you figure out what tool you can use in the *ACE Performance Workbook* to help you anchor the positive shots and experiences on the golf course. Then you can receive more good shots and sustain peak performance.

Or is your pattern of thinking to stay open to
each shot and see what is going to happen
Be Curious like a child??

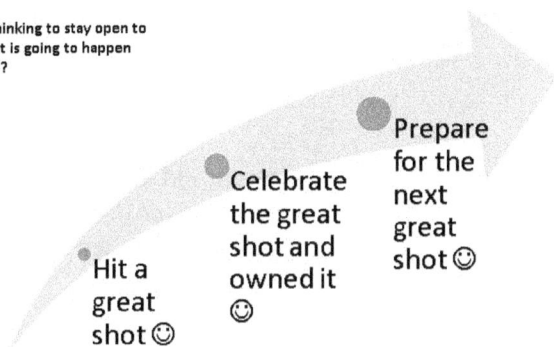

Prepare
for the
next
great
shot ☺

Celebrate
the great
shot and
owned it
☺

Hit a
great
shot ☺

Understanding your own golf cycle and your pattern of thoughts, emotions, actions, and anchors will be transformative in gaining more peak performances on the golf course. Like our beliefs and attitudes, our thinking can be a powerful force. Thinking and feeling are two leaves on the same branch. How we think affects how we feel, and how we feel affects how we perform.

Chapter 2 -ACE Performance Training Guide Homework

Go to Chapter Two **How Thoughts, Emotions, & Actions Dictate Your Golf Shots** in your guide and answer the reflective questions and complete the Golf Wheel exercise.

If you haven't already purchased and downloaded your copy of *The ACE Performance Training Guide*, you can get it here:

https://golf-thelastsixinches.com

CHAPTER 3

Golf is Mindful, Not Mindless:

Tools for Mindfulness on the Golf Course

"Your Beliefs become your thoughts.
Your thoughts become your words.
Your words become your actions.
Your actions become your habits.
Your habits become your values.
Your values become your destiny."

– Mahatma Gandhi

In this chapter, we are going deeper into understanding why mindfulness is so important for changing thoughts and actions, therefore, changing our golf game.

WHAT IS MINDFULNESS?

Mindfulness is a crucial element in the entire process of

your pre-shot and post-shot routines. It is a mental state achieved by focusing one's awareness on the present moment, while calmly acknowledging and accepting one's feelings, thoughts, and bodily sensations. The hardest shot in golf is the current one. So many times, golfers are not presently thinking about the current shot, many times they are thinking about the next shot, or the last shot. Understanding how to be present is essential to being mindful. Being mindful in this day and age is difficult because we have so many obstacles and distractions in our way. We have cell phones, computers, and televisions taking up space in our lives and minds. This busy, over-stimulated world trains our minds to be elsewhere and not in the present moment.

PRACTICING MINDFULNESS

Mindfulness is the practice of purposely focusing your attention on the present moment and accepting it without judgment.[3] Being mindful of your emotions are important because we are going to have many different emotions on the golf course. Coping with your emotions is key to creating and sustaining peak performances. We will be talking about acceptance in this chapter. Acceptance is a term used in mindfulness to help players understand their emotions and actions. Yes, emotions will be present, but what are you doing with them and how are you coping with that fearful state of mind while on the golf course? Being present on the golf course means you must be paying attention to the current shot you are about to hit not the last one or even the next one after this shot.

TEACHING YOURSELF TO BE MINDFUL

We always say awareness is the first step of change. This is why we ask that you go through *The ACE Performance*

---

[3] "What Is Mindfulness? - Meditation." Sharecare. Accessed October 7, 2015.

when it comes to identifying what you are focusing on, on and off the golf course.

BENEFITS OF JOURNAL WRITING

I feel there are at least five great reasons why journaling is one of the most important tools in peak performance.[5] It is the best way to understand our past, present, and future. In journaling, we can document our struggles, wins, and relationships with ourselves and others on and off the golf course.

Reason #1

Journals help us have a better connection with our thoughts, emotions, and goals. By journal writing, you better understand the relationship between what you believe in and why you believe in it. For example, let's say you are playing golf in a scramble event. You are next to a green side bunker and another player in your scramble team says we should chip this shot. Your first thought is, *"No, I should pitch this shot."* If you decided to pitch the shot and you performed it well, this is an example of what you should be writing in your journal. Write down why you did the pitch instead of a chip, why it worked for you, and what your thoughts were at the time you made that decision.

Writing in a journal helps you eliminate the mental clutter and you begin to learn how to get very clear about details on why you do what you do and feel what you feel. A journal will help you clarify your wishes, your dreams, and your goals.

Reason #2

Journals improve your overall focus and mental clarity

---

[5] "Journal Writing: 5 Smart Reasons Why YOU Should Start ..." 2015. 30 Sep. 2015 <http://www.lifehack.org/articles/communication/journal-writing-5-smart-reasons-why-you-should-start-doing-today.html>

which in turn help us help solve problems on the golf course. For example, you are in tight spot and not sure what technique or club to use in the situation. Clarity of the situation is crucial to performing the shot as you desire. How does this relate to using a journal? After the round, you can reflect on what was going on in your mind during that difficult situation. By writing about it, you can get clear what you would do next time you have that situation and you can learn how you can problem solve faster and more effectively.

If there's one thing journal writing is good for, it's clearing the mental clutter. How does it work? Whenever you have a problem and write about it in a journal, you transfer the problem from your head to the paper. This empties the mind, allowing allocation of precious resources to problem-solving rather than problem-storing.[6]

Reason #3

Journals improve insight and understanding. Why would you need insight and understanding in your golf game? First off, insight gives you critical thinking skills to ask the right questions about assessing your golf game. One must understand what they are doing correctly or incorrectly in any sport. As a positive consequence of improving your mental clarity, you become more open to insights you may have missed before. As you write your thoughts and emotional notes out, you're essentially having a conversation with yourself. This draws out insights that you would've missed otherwise; it's almost as if two people are working together to better understand each other. On the golf course, if you are not sure of a decision to make regarding a club selection or shot selection, having more insight gained from past experiences will help you problem solve. This kind of insight is only available to the person who

---

[6] "Journal Writing: 5 Smart Reasons Why YOU Should Start Doing It TODAY." Lifehack RSS. Accessed October 7, 2015.

has taken the time to connect with and understand themselves in the form of writing.

Once you've gotten a few entries written down, new insights can be gleaned from reading over them. You can look back on what you wrote and reflect on themes or patterns that are occurring in thoughts behaviors and language[7].

You might notice you are switching goals halfway through your rounds of golf or you might notice a pattern of self-talk occurring in certain situations. By capturing these events in writing, you become insightful in finding answers to your patterns of thinking, behaviors, or experiences.

Reason #4

Journals track your overall development and help you see your progressions. Life happens on the golf course, and sometimes we don't take the time to stop and look around at what's happening to us each round. So what happens? Round after round, it's the same story. Before you know it, you are having the same bad experiences on the golf course and you have no idea how that happens.

Journal writing allows us to see how we've changed over time, so we can see what and where we did things right, and we can see where we took a wrong turn, such as an incorrect decision on a shot or a club selection on a difficult shot. The great thing about journals is that you'll figure out where you might have had a similar experience, but you want a different outcome. Journaling allows you to learn from your mistakes.

Reason #5

Journals facilitate personal growth. Golf is the greatest sport in the world to really learn about ourselves, and the best thing about journal writing is that no matter what we end up

---

[7] "Journal Writing: 5 Smart Reasons Why YOU Should Start Doing It TODAY." Lifehack RSS. Accessed October 7, 2015.

writing about, it's hard to not learn something from our reflections and entries. You can look back and learn from experiences and decisions to pull your game forward toward your goals. The journal is a powerful tool because we gain so much personal growth from using one.

DIARY VERSUS PERFORMANCE JOURNAL

There are two different types of journals we are going to discuss: the diary journal and the performance journal.

A diary is what happens to you in life: the good, the bad, and the ugly. You can write down how you feel about things that have happened to you. It's like talking to your best friend, and they are just listening. A diary is a place where you write down what happened to you on the golf course. A diary is where you can dump out everything that happened that day on the golf course. You rewind the entire round. A diary is not a bad tool; however, if you want to shift and create more success in golf, you must use a performance journal.

A performance journal is a tool for performance. It's an assessment tool. The performance journal is about performance, not about what happened. You know what happened; you lived it that day on the golf course. The performance journal is a tool to be used to help you focus on your performance. Writing in the performance journal is about documenting the facts about your performances and what is good about your golf game. It is to help you stay focused on what you want.

The performance journal will have these questions in it:

- How did you execute shots today?
- What did you notice when you were playing great?
- What were thoughts when you played well or hit good shots?
- How did your body feel when you hit good shots?
- What was your self-talk when you were playing well or striking the golf ball well?

If you want to play better, you must pay attention to when you're playing well.

Remember, what you think about and talk about you tend to focus on. The probability of that happening in your golf game gets stronger. If you write about all the bad things that happened to you on the golf course, there will be more bad stuff that shows up in your game.

Again, the performance journal is about your performance. If you want to have a better life or better performances on the golf course, what you think about and what you write about, must be what you WANT, not what you DON'T WANT.

I give my clients a performance journal in which they have critical thinking questions to answer about their thoughts, emotions, and actions on the golf course.

In this performance journal, you will journal about your state of mind, or moods you are in, and what type of language you use with yourself. Journaling about your emotional patterns is no different that tracking the number of fairways hit in a round. It's an assessment tool to create a reflection and look at patterns to help you solve an issue that occurs while you play. You will also track your self-talk and reflect on how your language affects your golf game.

In my *Change Your Brain, Change Your Game* golf retreats, the first exercise we have our participants engage in is to go play four or five holes and write down everything we say or hear ourselves saying to ourselves. They chart their self-talk and really become mindful of what type of language they use during play. By writing down what you hear you will soon learn what type of language you use on yourself. Journaling will teach you awareness of your self-talk. You might just realize what type of friend or not so good of a friend you are to yourself on the golf course. Are you your own best friend out on the golf course or do you only give all your own best friend advice out to others like most golfers tend to do? Journaling your self-talk will reveal what type of relationship you really have with yourself on the golf course.

If you want something to change, the first step of change is awareness. Journaling is a great tool for awareness, and it's a must in my practice of coaching. Most people keep doing the same thing over and over again and expecting different results.

That's how Einstein defined insanity! Yet, we do that in golf many times. We play poorly, and go straight to the range, or go take a full swing lesson because we think we need to fix something broken with our technique. You can change your strategy and become more aware of how you are feeling and how you are thinking on the golf course. Journaling will help you become more aware of your thoughts before, during, and after the round.

Some people journal during rounds, some people journal after rounds; it doesn't matter. You get to choose what works best for you. The key is to become aware and mindful of how you are feeling and how you are treating yourself. You might start to notice what shows up for you and when.

By being mindful and presently aware you can notice what you focus on, and you can notice how your body feels and reacts. You might start to notice a pattern occurring. Great news, once you know your pattern, you know you can change it by using different strategies instead of the definition of insanity strategy. Journaling is so powerful because it is when you are writing things down that it gets anchored in your subconscious.

Research tells us that if you are writing things down, the kinesthetic response in the body bypasses these thoughts into the subconscious.[8] If you are writing more about the negative experiences in your life or what's wrong with your life, or golf game, then you are giving negative energy more fuel, therefore, we focus on those experiences more. If we write down what we want in our lives or our golf game, then that's more likely to occur as well. It teaches us how to rewire our subconscious. Journaling is a space where you can dump out all the bad stuff; however, it is so much more important to write about what you

---

[8] Purcell, M. (2013). The Health Benefits of Journaling. *Psych Central*.

want and focus on what you want.

After writing in the journal for a week, you should go back and reflect on what you wrote about. What showed up more? Was it all the negative stuff in your golf game or was it more positive events in your golf game?

When writing this book, it took me a long time to settle in and start writing because I had many thoughts about the what ifs, and that prevented me from writing this book. It has taken two years because I had a story in my head that my knowledge wasn't enough to be heard or my expertise isn't enough to make a difference. It was only after I started writing in my journal that I realized I was self-sabotaging my own journey of becoming a Best Selling Author. I started reading my journal entries and noticed all my entries were about what was wrong with my life and why I did not have my book done. It was very surreal reading back over what I wrote in the journal.

I started to write down what I wanted to happen, not what I was afraid was going to happen. Things changed, I started believing in myself, I started to manifest better clients, and my business and life turned around. The only shift that occurred to help me facilitate my completion of this book was journal writing. I stayed focused on what I wanted and didn't worry about when the book was going to get done. I just kept focused on the process of writing and feeling good about the process. It took a while before I felt good about the process of writing. Journaling really helped turn that around for me.

Journaling is a great tool because it allows you to become mindful and reflective. After reflecting, you can start to come up with better solutions in your thinking. Once you are clear with what you want in your golf game, then you can shift your actions and come up with better strategies and solutions. In *Change your Brain, Change your Game* workshops and seminars, you learn how to start thinking differently and treating yourself differently. From a different state of mind you create different strategies to get what you want. This is when things start to change.

ACE Performance Training
Guide Homework

Go to Chapter Three **Golf is Mindful, Not Mindless: Tools for Mindfulness on the Golf Course** in your guide and answer the reflective questions and complete the Halfway to Meditation breathing exercise.

If you haven't already purchased and downloaded your copy of *The ACE Performance Training Guide,* you can get it here:

http://golf-thelastsixinches.com

CHAPTER 4

Where Your Focus Goes, The Shots Will Go

*Focus, darn it! Concentrate on
keeping your head down.*

*Focus on your left arm.
You need to think scoring low today.*

"Where focus goes, energy flows."

– Tony Robbins

Do you hear yourself saying some of these things on the golf course? No matter what you say to yourself, your focus doesn't seem to help your golf game.

Focus is defined as the center of interest, attraction, or attention to an activity. This chapter will help you understand how clear your focus is and what you are paying attention to in your golf game. We will be using terms like attention, awareness, and focus synonymously in this chapter. Focus is very powerful. It's a gift we choose to utilize or not. We have control over what we focus on. In golf, we know there are many things we can't control. You can't control other players, the weather, the length of the putting green, etc. Isn't it nice to know that we do have control over something out there called our own focus? We get to choose what we decide to feel, how we want to swing, what club we want. That decision is powerful, so just decide what you want to focus on. If you choose to blame others or the course conditions for your poor performance, then you have decided to play poorly. You have chosen that. You can't hide or run away from yourself. You are the one on the golf course. Your abilities, your choices, your decisions, your attitude; it is you, not your golf swing.

What you FOCUS on, you will FEEL. When your focus changes, your emotions change. This creates a shift for a better golf game and even a better life. When you change your focus, you can immediately change your state of mind or how you feel in the moment.

What do you want to focus on? Here is where you need to be honest with yourself because if you are not honest with yourself, you will not make any changes. The most important factor to change is to have an honest acceptance as to where you are in your golf game. What's your personal truth in your putting, long game, short game, etc.? What type of conversation are you having in your head?

The conversations you have inside your own mind come from what you focus on and your belief systems. You have the freedom to direct your mind to give every shot a chance, whether it is a putt, a driver off the tee, or sand shot. The key is to constantly move in the direction of what you **DO WANT**. The best players in the world still miss shots; however, the difference between that championship golfer and an amateur is that the championship golfer always, always, gives the ball a chance to go in.

- Do you trust yourself and what you have trained yourself to do?
- What have you trained yourself to do? Make or miss more putts?
- Have you trained yourself to give yourself a chance every time you strike the ball?

Dr. Bob Rotella teaches his players in his book, *Putting Like a Genius,*[9] to make the putting green you are putting on today the type of putting green you absolutely love, no matter the speed, or the elevations, or the length of the greens. He states, "Make today's putting green your favorite no matter the conditions. You get to choose." That is a different focus than thoughts like, "Oh my gosh, the green speed is a 12 today. I can't putt on these greens!"[10] Then your focus goes to missing putts because you are afraid of the speed of the green. Again, what are you focusing on?

In golf, people talk about focus every day. Some people say their focus is to have a good time or just play well, or they may say something like, "I want to focus on beating my opponent."

Paying attention to your focus is the first step towards mental toughness and peak performance. Becoming aware of your focus is helpful in assessing your roadmap to mental toughness. The when and what you are focusing on are critical to changing your golf game and your life. You may be thinking you can focus on the golf course. However, do you really know what you are focused on? You plan to focus on making three foot putts. You start by making three foot putts, then you start to miss, and you begin to focus on your mechanics. Oh no, here comes the change of focus. No longer are you focusing on making putts because your mind is focused on how you are bringing the putter back. Thoughts start popping in your head, "*Is the putter blade square? Am I swinging inside out or outside in on my swing path?*"

The floodgates open, and all these thoughts come rushing in during your practice. Then you get lost in your practice, you lose focus, and the entire practice time is wasted. You are no longer focused on making three foot putts because you turned

[9] Rotella, Dr. Robert. Putting Like a Genius. Simon & Schuster Audio, 2010.

[10] Rotella, Robert J., and Robert Cullen. Golf Is Not a Game of Perfect. New York: Simon & Schuster, 1995.

your attention to mechanical practice mode. The result is you are no longer you making three footers. This is where your change of focus will change your emotions. Yes, focusing on the wrong thing at the wrong time can and will hurt your golf game. Just like in life, you get what you think about whether you want it or not. Whatever we focus on expands and gets bigger in our minds.

> *"When you set your tuner to a station, you're going to hear what's playing. Whatever you are focused upon is the way you set your tuner, and when you focus there for as little as 17 seconds, you activate that vibration within you. Once you activate a vibration within you, the Law of Attraction begins responding to that vibration, and you're off and running—whether it's something wanted or unwanted."*

– Abraham-Hicks

When we play golf, we tend to be easily distracted by all the external factors, such as other playing partners, golf course conditions, and speed of the greens. We tend to lose ourselves like a car without GPS. When we focus on the distractions, we get lost and make poor decisions. What we focus on is what we end up with.

An example of this is when you are on the golf course and you are on a tee box. You start looking down the fairway and at bunkers on both sides. Where does your focus immediately go? Be honest! Do you automatically start thinking thoughts such as:

> *"Don't go in those bunkers because I will never get out of them."*
> *"Ok, let's see here, I want to hit the fairway, but be careful of bunker on the left."*

Your brain hears bunker, bunker, bunker, and that is where

your focus goes. You are giving more energy to the bunkers than anything else at that moment.

For the first 17 seconds, guess what you are not focused on? I would put money on it that you are focused on where you **don't want** to hit the ball. Unfortunately, those thoughts are directing your brain to focus there. Our brain can't delineate the difference between **do and don't**. The brain sees and hears the bunker; therefore, it focuses on the bunker. Where does the shot go? Into the bunker.

HOW LONG SHOULD WE FOCUS?

Persistence leads to a shift. Research tells us if you focus from 17 to 68 seconds, your thoughts are creating energy. Abraham-Hicks describes focus within the Law of Attraction in this way:

> *That energy is attracting what you are focused upon. WITH ONLY A FEW SECONDS of focusing your attention on a subject, you activate the vibration of that subject within you, and immediately the Law of Attraction begins to respond to that activation. The longer you keep your attention focused on something, the easier it becomes for you to continue to focus upon it because you are attracting other thoughts or vibrations that are the essence of the thought you began with.*[11]

Within 17 seconds of focusing on something, such as a cup on the putting green, a matching vibration becomes activated. Now, as that focus becomes stronger and the vibration becomes clearer, the Law of Attraction will bring to you more thoughts that match. At this point, the vibration will not have much attraction power, but if you maintain your focus longer, the power of the vibration will become further reaching.

---

[11] "Abraham-Hicks." Abraham-Hicks. Accessed October 7, 2015.

If you manage to stay purely focused upon any thought for as little as 68 seconds, the vibration is powerful enough that its manifestation begins. We use this tool to manifest positive self-talk affirmations as well.

Putting example:

If you are staying focused on making, and believing you are going to make, three footers for more than 68 seconds, your emotional belief changes and you begin to manifest the belief of making three footers.

When you repeatedly return to a pure thought such as, *"I can make three footers,"* maintaining it for at least 68 seconds, in a short period of time (hours in some cases or a few days in others), that thought becomes a dominant thought.

Many people focus on where they don't want the golf ball to end up. It's very critical to focus on what you want versus what you don't want on the golf course. Start paying attention to what your fixed point of focus is while you play. Do you look at your fixed point of interest, such as the water or the sand, or the middle of the fairway? Again, your brain doesn't know the difference between **DO and DON'T.** It only hears and focuses on the fixed point of interest and where most of your thought energy is taking you. This is where you are directing your brain to take your body.

As the vibration or focus gets stronger, your personal GPS system is signaling your nervous system to make a swing toward the bunker. On the golf course, you are standing on a tee box on a par three, and your focus goes directly to the bunker on the left of the green. That focus is actual energy. When your focus goes to some object like a bunker or a lake or even the green, that is where your attention goes. This may or may not be your target, but to your mind, wherever your attention goes, that image will be your mind's target. You must be mindful as to where your focus or attention is because those are the directions you are giving your body to swing towards. If your focus is on a bunker, then there is a good chance that is where the golf ball will end up - in the bunker. It is the same concept as when you plug driving directions into your GPS system of your car. It takes you where you direct it to go.

Your thoughts are very powerful energy forces. You need to practice on how, what, and when you focus.

You have the ability to direct
your thoughts on the golf course.
You get what you think about,
whether you want it or not.

You have the ability to direct your own thoughts; you have the option of observing things as they are, or of imagining them as you want them to be. Whether you are imagining or observing, your focus is equally powerful. You have the option of remembering something as it actually occurred or imagining it as you would prefer. You have the option of remembering something that pleased you or remembering something that did not please you. You have the option of anticipating something you want or anticipating something you do not want.

In every case, your thoughts produce a vibration within you that equals your point of attraction, and then circumstances and events line up to match the vibrations that you have offered. Just like in the case of you looking down the fairway when your focus goes to the bunkers on both sides of the fairway. You may not even know your attention goes to the bunkers or other obstacles on the golf course.[12]

I have a client who came to me wanting to create a change in her golf game, and she heard I could help with her mindset. This player was a good mechanical player ranging handicap from 8-12 most days. However, in tournament play, she would show up as a 20 handicap or worse.

Her anxiety level before and during competitive events was

---

[12] "Disappearance of the Universe Quote for Today." KEEN: : Law of Attraction. Accessed October 7, 2015.

at an all time high. The first topic of discussion was her focus. We went directly to what she was focusing on in her golf game. It was clear she was full of worry and doubt about what other people thought of her. Her focus was on the worry about not being good enough and what if her "A" game didn't show up. Her main focus was on variables she had no control over, for example other people's feelings and thoughts. Her main focus was the story in her head. What if she didn't play well? We talked about why she liked to play golf and she gave me the following reasons:

I love to be outside.
I love playing with my friends.
I love the game because it's a great sport for me to be active and to still feel like an athlete.

After listing her WHY's, I simply told her, "Let's focus on these great statements. Your self-talk can be like this when you play golf:

I love being out here today.
I love being with my best friends playing this great game.
I love playing this game with my friends.

That's it. Nothing more, nothing less. If you change your focus, you can change your state of mind. The strategy was to bring her back to her WHY she played the game. Instead of worrying about what others think or the what ifs, we talked about focusing on what we could control - ourselves and our thoughts. We reconnected her with her big WHY.

Staying connected to your WHY, as we discussed in Chapter 1, will change your focus. As she stayed connected to her WHY, her focus changed. She started having new thoughts and feelings about how it felt being with her friends. Having fun gave her feelings of love, caring, peace, and joy. These emotions changed her emotional state. She felt better about herself because she learned how to stay engaged with her

WHY. Changing your focus will change your emotional state every time. Just be careful what you focus on. Just like focusing on the bunker will cause a shift in your emotional state. I would bet those emotions probably will not be love, joy, and happiness when you find yourself in the bunker.

She gave herself permission to be loved by others and learned how to accept compliments from other players. It started to create a shift and transformed her golf game and her life. Her belief of being worthy of these compliments helped create that shift. She created a vibration of happiness and love in herself, and she created better golf shots and better experiences on the golf course.

Loving thy self gives you
more love to pay forward.

MOOD STATES

We talk about mood states in coaching. You play your best when you feel your best. There are two different mood states. Your emotions, or mood states, are either low or high grade. My client was having low vibrational states or emotions because her thoughts were generating those low-grade states. She changed her thoughts and changed her emotional state, and learned how to feel better before and during her rounds of golf. She learned these high-grade thoughts were helpful in her everyday life as well.

Low Vibration/ Grade States	High Vibration/ Grade States
Anger	Joy
Intimidation	Happy
Sadness	Blissful
Anxious	Excited
Fearful	Loving
Trying	Trusting

Tense	Brave
Tightness	Relaxed

**You can always change your state
by changing what you are focusing on.**

HOW CAN YOU CHANGE YOUR STATE OF EMOTIONS?

You can change the state of your emotions by focusing back on WHY you are playing this game. If you are frustrated, then you are not connected or engaged in your WHY. You may have lost your reasons to play and other distractions have creeped in and your focus is different. The golf game is now giving you back your expected outcomes because they don't match your WHYs.

CONNECTING YOUR WHY TO YOUR FOCUS

You started to play golf, and your intention of the day was to enjoy the round with your friends. You start to play and find out one of your friends is bringing in another player. This player is very competitive in nature and very focused on the score. That player keeps asking you, "What did you shoot on that hole?" Remember, you were just going to play a fun round of golf. You can see how this player can distract you from your WHY and you start worrying about your shots, your score, how you look to them, etc. Did you all of sudden start trying to beat your playing partner even though you original WHY was to have an enjoyable round of golf? Did you shift your focus to the competition? Either your focus changed and/or other external or internal distractions changed your focus for you. It's easy to do.

Don't let anyone take your focus away from you. Stay connected to your WHY, and you will feel better and play better. Play your game, whatever that is for the day or round. You get to decide what to focus on, not anyone else. Stay connected to your plan of enjoyment. Find ways to enjoy the game, even though someone else might be trying to take you off your game. People will try to, and situations will come up that will, take your focus away. Even in life, people ask things of you every day, and it is hard to stay focused on your plan and your goals. We stay connected to our WHY so we stay engaged and our focus can stay on track. If your state of mind/focus changes throughout your game, your emotions will change.

THE FRONT 9 - BACK 9 SYNDROME

I came up with this term because I hear stories all the time of players telling me, "I played well the front nine and the back nine went to the birds," or, "I played horribly the front nine and the back nine I was a rock star." How does this happen?

Ask yourself and pay attention to what caused the shift in performance between front and back nine. We have all have had not so good days on the golf course. Let's say your front nine was horrible and you could hear yourself say, *"Oh wow, I am not playing well today,"* or, *"I knew I wasn't going to play well today."* These self-sabotaging thoughts create your reality. Like we stated earlier, thought precedes emotion, emotions precede behavior. That is a great example of self- fulfilling prophecy in golf.

You have a thought, you start believing it, and you start living it on the golf course. Your focus equals your reality. *"Oh, I can't wait to get this round over with. The wheels have fallen off,"* or, *"Man, do I need a drink at the turn."* Then you get to the turn, and a shift occurs. Something caused the shift, either a drink or maybe acceptance of who you were that day or you started to give up on TRYING to play well. Once you stop trying, then you start playing well. Hence, the Front nine Back nine Syndrome.

So why do you start playing well?

- You might start to accept you for who you are that day and something caused your focus to shift to a different thought. Maybe even a beverage at the turn created the change of focus.

- Sometimes just knowing you get to start over on the back nine causes you to shift your focus.

Alternatively, you might play very well on the front nine and you are having a career round. What happens on the back nine? You start playing poorly. WHY?

Is it because your thoughts have changed? You might think, *"Oh my, if I continue to play this well, I am going to break my career best,"* or, *"Wow, where is this coming from, I don't ever play this well."* Self-sabotaging thoughts start to run your golf game. Emotions start to shift. These thoughts are not the same thoughts or focus you were having on the front nine when you were playing well. Many people jump into the future and start focusing on what might happen, and that is not the same state of mind that they were in when they were playing on the front nine. Hence, the focus changes, then emotions change, and finally, the performance changes. The past is gone and the future is not here yet. Forget the past and live breathe and play in the present. The future is not here yet, so stop worrying about it.

You get what you focus upon. It is Law.
Your golf game is a result of what you focus upon.

When you hit a great shot, do you pay attention to your great shots, or do you focus on when you struggled or played poorly? Most players focus on what's wrong with their golf game, not what is right with their golf game. Traditional golf instruction focuses on fixes and concentrates on what's wrong with someone's golf swing, such as mechanics.

What if we started paying attention when you play well?

Can you think of a time you played well? What thoughts were you having when you played well? How do you feel when you are playing well? People ask me often, "How do I get to play in the zone and stay in the zone? There are rounds of golf I play very well, while other times I play like I have never picked up a club before!" If you want to keep playing well, then start paying attention to what are you doing, how are you feeling, and what emotions come up for you when you are successful.

YOUR "MUST" FOR FOCUS

Imagine going to play a new course you have never played before. It's just you, no one else is playing with you. Most of the time, it's easy to focus on where to go. You pick a spot on the fairway, and you swing to place the ball there. In another scenario, you are playing a new course, but this time you are with members who have played there many times. They give you the entire low down of the course, telling you everything about the hole layout, where not to go, or what to avoid. With all that information overload, where does your attention start to flow?

Most people would start to focus on where not to go based on the members' descriptions. Good players know how to eliminate these distractions and focus in on their intended target. This is called narrowed focus, and you can develop this skill for peak performance on the golf course.

Highly skilled athletes, including golfers, have two types of focus. One is called narrow and the other is broad focus. In golf, you have a lot to focus on, but what you focus on will help you perform better. The "MUST" of focus is called narrow focus. **Narrow focus** is defined as a clear, vivid image in your brain you have on a target. Narrow focus is when you pay attention to a specific part of your target. The better the image of your intended target you give to your brain, the more energy you are giving yourself to tune in on it. The clearer the image, the increased chance your brain locks in on the that target and the better chance your body will make the correct swing to take the ball to that intended target. **Broad focus** would be when you can see the green, you see the bunker left, and water right of the green. You see everything on and around the green.

In golf, you want to have both broad and narrow focus. However, when you are ready to hit a shot, you only want a clear vivid image in your mind of where you want the golf ball to go. Stay focused on what you want to do. You should be stating out loud and verbally, "I want to go there," and be very specific about where. This takes practice because we tend to focus on where we don't want to go.

- Narrow focus means, you look down the fairway, and you see a tree behind your target on the green. You actually can see the leaf on the tree branch that aligns with the intended outcome. Broad focus would be looking around the fairway paying attention to what is out there where you don't want to swing towards.

- With narrow focus, you are looking at the cup on the green and your intended aim is the green blade of grass that is at 10 O'clock position on the cup. Broad focus would be focusing on hitting the putt just to the hole.

Can you think of any other types of narrow focus which might help you understand this concept?

Different focus, different results...It's a mindset.

PROCESS AND OUTCOME THINKERS

Understanding what focus is all about in golf is important so you know what to focus on. To be great at any sport, or anything in life, you must first be a process thinker. You must be mindful of the process to get you where you want to go. Let's explain the difference between process and outcome thinkers.

Great performers are process oriented thinkers, not outcome thinkers. Yes, great athletes have goals for being the best; however, they are very mindful of the process to get to that peak performance level.

When you play golf, are you a process thinker or an outcome thinker?

A process thinker is one who is mindful of their process of what they are doing in the caddy box, play box and post-shot routines. They have a system and routines to help them stay process oriented when they play. These processes help them achieve their outcome goals.

An outcome thinker is one who thinks about the score which is something you can't control completely. Outcome thinkers will have thoughts such as, *"Well, if I play well the next three holes, I will score my personal best,"* or *"Well, if I just make this birdie, I will be club champion."* Thoughts like these take you out of the present moment.

MECHANICAL VERSUS TARGET FOCUS

Training your mechanics is a great way to improve your golf game. However, if you are focused on mechanics when you play golf, you will not be successful at hitting your target because that is not what you are focused on. Are you focused on grip, stance, posture, or the ball going to the target? You can't focus on your swing mechanics if you want to move the ball to the target.

For example, you are going to hit a 27 yard wedge shot on the golf course. After you collected the data on yardage, lie, green contour, and target, what do you do next? Where does your focus go, to the mechanics of the shot or do you focus on the 27 yards you need to carry the shot? What is your fixed point of interest in this shot?

If you look at the wedge, the ball, or the ground as you take some practice swings, you will immediately focus on your swing mechanics. Your brain will go to thoughts like, *"Oops, I chunked that last swing, and I better not do that again."* You'll have thoughts like, *"Wonder how far should I take this club back now."* Should you be thinking about mechanics while playing?

If you focus on mechanics, you will get mechanics. Your brain will focus on what your thoughts are telling it to focus on. If you focus on mechanics, your eyes are no longer on the target, and you can't feel the distance of a 27 yard swing. Your brain doesn't know it even exists any longer. The 27 yard shot target is gone, and the outcome will not be a good shot because you lost the feel of it focusing on the mechanics of the shot.

Practicing mechanics and focusing on a target are two completely different concepts. Playing golf means trusting your mechanical training. On the golf course, you collect data, trust, and respond. Playing means trusting yourself and executing. Golf is a target sport. Look at your target and respond to it. That is it.

Practicing is about training and playing is about trusting.

Training your confidence should never ever depend on whether you execute the shot. You should not have to see it to believe it. You need to believe it before you see it. Training yourself to focus on your confidence before the shot or putt is crucial to peak performance. It's very critical to focus on what you want versus what you don't want on the golf course.

SUMMARY OF FOCUS STRATEGIES

Before Your Shots:

1. Don't wait until your performance tells you that you should feel better. Don't wait for good outcomes to let you feel great. Don't wait for exceptional scores to allow yourself to feel exceptional.

2. Don't wait to feel your best. Feel great right now and

change your state of mind.

3. You can view the golf course as it is, nothing more, nothing less. Accept what is, and play as it lies.

4. Imagine the golf course or golf shot as you want it to be. Start by being creative in your mind. What do you really want out of this situation?

5. Focus on your confidence. Trust your training and coaching.

6. Peak performance is knowing and trusting that you will give this shot a chance.

7. Go on vacation in your mind to help you stay emotionally free and open. The higher emotional vibration you create will give you what you want. Find the joy in your heart before striking that putt.

8. Trying less will get you what you want. Trying harder to focus will frustrate you.

Remember That:

- "What we focus on EXPANDS both positive and negative.
- The thoughts you think equal your point of attraction.
- You get what you think about, whether you want it or not.
- Your thoughts equal vibration, and that vibration is then answered by the Law of Attraction.
- As your vibration expands and becomes more powerful, it eventually becomes powerful enough to manifest what you desire."[13](Abraham-Hicks)

>>>>>YOUR NEXT STEP >>>>>

---

[13] "Abraham-Hicks." Abraham-Hicks. Accessed October 7, 2015.

Chapter 4 - ACE Performance Training Guide Homework

Go to Chapter Four **Where Your Focus Goes, Your Shots Will Go** in your journal and answer the reflective questions and complete the Key exercise.

If you haven't already purchased and downloaded your copy of ***The ACE Performance Training Guide,*** you can get it here:

http://golf-thelastsixinches.com

CHAPTER 5

Your Words Equal Your Beliefs

*"When I let go of what I am,
I become what I might be."*

– Lao Tzu

SELF-TALK

Understanding our language is a great way to gain not only insight, but access to the subconscious mind and our underlying beliefs. No matter who we are, how we speak to ourselves not only reflects, but affects every aspect of our golf and life. What we tell ourselves on an ongoing basis, whether it be good or bad, right or wrong, reflects not only what we think, but also how we feel and act. This can directly influence our results on and off the golf course.

Observing the language we use may help us become more aware of what is happening inside our head and also to understand how those thoughts are directly linked to creating our reality. By taking notice of our language, both internally and externally, we gain awareness. The more aware we are of what we are saying, the more successful we can be in every area of our golf game and life[14].

WHAT IS SELF-TALK?

Your self-talk is how you talk about yourself to yourself, both internally and externally, on the golf course. Self-talk is a concept that happens in both the pre-shot and post-shot routines. Self-talk can direct your state of mind and your physical state.

I have many players who speak to themselves very poorly on the golf course. They talk as if they really hated themselves. They would say statements like, "Well, that was stupid of me," or, "Oh, you are such an idiot!"

Here is an example of a player and her self-talk discovery. We will name this player Jackie. Jackie came to me for help with her golf game, so the first variable we addressed was her self-talk. I went out and played nine holes with her. I just listened to her external self-talk and noticed how she was treating herself on the golf course. After the round, we sat down and I listed all the type of words she was using while talking about her shots. Those words were not friendly words. We went through the list of words she used with herself and also some of the statements she would say before and after shots. Phrases like:

Trying to hit this shot, but...
What if I don't...

Some of her self-talk statements when she played in competition were:

"I am not good enough to play with these other players....I am not worthy of winning."
"OMG, what if I blow up and can't shoot my handicap? My partner is going to be mad at me if I don't play well."
"What will people think of me when I don't perform?"
"What if I embarrass myself?"

Jackie found out through her self-talk assessments that she

---

[14] "Thoughts - Mind-Sets." MindSets. Accessed October 7, 2015.

was beating herself up and focusing on the negative aspects of her game, not the positives at all. The negative self-talk heavily outweighed the positive self-talk statements. The first step was to help her become self-aware of how she was treating herself on the golf course. What did she say to herself? We focused on the language and meanings that were happening inside her own head before, during, and after play. She found out that she focused on all the negative thoughts or the what ifs worse case scenarios while she played. All her thoughts and self-talk were very disempowering and paralyzed her play. Her negative self-talk and thoughts were causing her to play in fear and heightened stress levels. She would have so much anxiety, she would actually feel sick to her stomach at times. Her negative thoughts were causing her throat to feel like it was closing up and her breathing was limited. She even felt panic attacks coming on before she played.

During our sessions, we talked about understanding what she was saying to herself and the story in her head before events. Once she realized how she beat herself up and how she showed up mentally, she was amazed. She definitely didn't like it, and she didn't like the way she was treating herself because she doesn't treat other people like that. She is very friendly and fun to play with. Her country club members love playing with her.

She knows in her heart she is a good person and everyone loves playing with her, but she built this story in her head through negative self talk and started to have anxiety around that story. After journaling her self-talk for a few rounds, she realized she didn't like the relationship she was having with herself. After further discussion, her awakening was when she started to realize was that she never accepted, or what I call "owned," any positive compliments other players would give her. She never gave herself any credit for good or great shots on the golf course. Even when she hit great shots, she did not own them or give herself the high fives, physically or even verbally with internal self-talk, she gave other players when they hit the same great shot.

- What is your self-talk before the round of play?
- What is your self-talk during play?
- What is your self-talk after you play?

We want to know the pattern so we can analyze where non-peak performances are showing up in your game.

HOW IMPORTANT IS SELF-TALK?

Very important because it begins our golf performance cycle. Remember, our thoughts and self-talk create our emotions on the golf course, and our emotions create our actions and decisions.

The internal self-talk is the inner voice you hear in your head, and external self-talk is what you actually verbalize about yourself out loud before and after shots. Most people have both internal self-talk and external self-talk, but not everyone. Some people never verbalize their self-talk, and others you hear talking to themselves the entire round.

MANAGING YOUR SELF-TALK

First, you must become fully aware of your self-talk. I have my players journal their internal and external conversations with themselves while they play six to nine holes of golf. It doesn't take long to figure out what their patterns of language are because what they usually do in their life will show up on the golf course as well.

After writing down their patterns of language, we discuss in our workshops some ways to manage that self-talk. They must understand that their self-talk comes from their beliefs system in their subconscious.

You must learn how to focus on creating a statement of desire. What do you really want? This is where the journaling really helps you get clear. Remember, you want to give your subconscious the right statement of vision so it can work for you, not against you.

Repeat after me:

I am a poor putter...I am a poor putter... I am a poor putter... I am a poor putter.

How does that feel? Do you think this is a statement of desire? I don't think so, but if you say that to yourself then you start to believe it and you wire it in your subconscious. You start becoming a poor putter because you actually believe it.

Now this time say this statement out loud:

I am a great putter. I am a great putter. I am a great putter. I am a great putter.

Say it out loud a couple of times; keep saying it. If you can't say great putter, say good putter. By changing the statements, I want you to feel more juiced up on who you really are. Give your statements some attitude!

Your statements will come out as to who you really are versus who you think you are. I know this sounds a little crazy. You must create a shift in your language to start creating a shift in your body and nervous system. Then you can you can re-wire the thoughts. The statements to start telling your body a different story.

If you keep telling yourself you are a horrible putter, then you will start to believe it, and that is what you end up focusing on. That will be the outcome you receive from your mindset.

GOAL SETTING AND LANGUAGE EXERCISE

What do you want out of your golf? How do you want your golf to be? What type of relationship would you want with yourself?

In setting a goal, the language you use is very important.

Your goal should be specific and in the present tense. Avoid I am going to... or I want to... statements. *"I want to be a better golfer."* This statement is not specific enough. What would it mean to be a better golfer? Let's be specific. A certain handicap. Putting less than two putts on greens.

Change it to be specific, and then change the statement to *"I am"*. By just changing your language, you can change your state. If you said to yourself, *"I want to be a better golfer."* What's does better mean to you? Be specific... What does better look like to you?

How does that actually feel to you? Good, bad, neutral? What if you change the statement to *"I am a great putter"*? When you say you want to be a better putter, you really don't believe you are a good putter. Wanting something tells the subconscious that you don't have this yet. Your subconscious reinforces this statement *"I can't putt."* If you change the statement to *"I am a good putter,"* and you start to say this statement with some emotion behind it, you start to believe it.

If you get to have everything you want in your golf game or your golf experience, what would that be? What would that look like? How would you feel if you reached your goals? At the end of this chapter, you'll have the opportunity to go to your *ACE Performance Journal* to complete the Goal Setting Exercise.

VAK EXERCISE AND THE WHOLE BRAIN BALANCE POSTURE

I use a Psych-K VAK exercise to help my players communicate directly with their subconscious mind to shift old self-limiting beliefs into new self-enhancing ones that support them. VAK exercise stands for Visual, Auditory and Kinesthetic. The Whole Brain Balance Posture is a process to create a balanced communication between both right and leftbrain hemispheres. This whole brain state is ideal for reprogramming the mind with new self-enhancing beliefs.

Once you find your whole brain balance posture (a process that must be facilitated by a certified PSYCH- K professional) then you work through creating your new belief statement.

Once you define what you want and you create a true "I am" statement, then you begin the whole brain integration to shift old limiting beliefs. The VAK exercise stimulates the visual, auditory, and kinesthetic sensory modalities of your nervous system. For more information on Psych- K, the work of Robert Williams and Dr. Bruce Lipton, check out the references in the back of this book.[15]

One of my clients used to always run to the tee box barely breathing and fully of anxiety because she was always rushing. She always beat herself up emotionally because she was often late, always rushing, and never starting off the round very well. We sat down and I asked her what she wanted. Rushing and being late was not her goal to start her rounds of golf. Her self-talk was always negative and she could hear herself saying statements like, *"Why am I always late?"* and *"Why do I feel so anxious on the first tee?"*

She went through the Whole Brain Balance Posture and VAK exercise. During the exercise, she realized that she was worried about what other people thought of her if she took the time to warm up; therefore, she never did. Her desire was to warm up and feel good about herself before she met players on the first tee. She was not showing up that way. During the VAK exercise, she created a new belief statement on what she really wanted for herself and now she takes time to warm up because she wants to take care of her needs first before she plays. She never felt like she deserved to take care of herself because she was worried about other people and how they think of her if she warmed up and took care of her needs first. Now, after the VAK exercise, she feels much better about herself, she takes her time for herself by properly warming up, and the anxiety

---

[15] Lipton, Bruce H. The Biology of Belief: Unleashing the Power of Consciousness, Matter & Miracles. Carlsbad, Calif.: Hay House, 2008.

goes away and never creeps back in. She now goes to the first tee in an empowered state of mind

HOW THE VAK EXERCISE WORKS

You will first want to create a strong "I am" statement before starting the whole brain balance posture. For example: "I *am a great putter on my golf course.*" Once you have a clear "I am" statement, sit back in a chair, get relaxed, and close your eyes. Now, interlock your fingers and place your hands on your lap comfortably. Notice which thumb is on top. Next, cross your legs at the ankles and notice which ankle is on top. We are checking in with your brain right now. Remember, the left side of your brain is controlling the right side of your body, and your right side controls the left side of your body. Whatever your whole brain balance posture is, you want to be in that posture or position when you are practicing and concentrating on new belief statements.

Just think about your new statement of belief. As you are sitting there, relaxed and just thinking about your new belief statement, what it looks like to you, what you see yourself doing, performing, or acting like? What do you see when you see yourself as in your new belief statement?

Let's say you are out on the golf course, what do you see yourself doing when you are there in your new belief statement? What would you be wearing? What do you see around you? What do you notice about the day or the scenery? How would you be on the tee box, or in the fairways, or onto or off the greens? How would you show up on the tee box once you have this new belief in your body? How would it feel once you have achieved your new belief statement? How does your body feel? What do you notice about your body or how any senses are enlightened or engaged? How you would celebrate it within your body? What would you be doing once you achieved it? What would you hear other people saying to you or about you when they see you achieve your new belief or goal?

Just be in it for a bit. What do you feel like? Did you notice any colors show up while you were sitting there being in it? What does your body feel like right now? What are you noticing? What does it feel like? Does this feel soft, round, square, warm, hot, or cold? Where in your body do you feel this?

Just notice.

Take a couple deep breaths and place the tips of your fingers of both hands together and just relax, and let that feeling be anchored into you for a bit. This is a STATE of mind that builds trust and feelings of safety with no judgement. This state is where the magic happens and you can create unlimited possibilities. How would that feel on the golf course? That avatar, that human being, is in you because you just created and anchored it. It is who you really are as a person, as a human being.

Practice being in that state. Practice daily, either in a chair, or even right before you fall asleep at night. That is a great time for your subconscious to let it in and anchor it. You have a choice as to what state you want to be in. Your state is who you are at that moment and how you show up. Who do you want to be, who are you and what do you want in every moment of your life? How are you going to treat yourself before or after swinging or playing?[16]

The key about this VAK exercise is to help you realize you can create the state to get you what you really want. It all starts with asking the right questions. At the end of this chapter, you'll have the opportunity to go to your *ACE Performance Journal* to complete the VAK Exercise.

> *"The quality of your questions
> is the quality of your life."*

– Anthony Robbins

[16] Lipton, Bruce H. The Biology of Belief: Unleashing the Power of Consciousness, Matter & Miracles. Carlsbad, Calif.: Hay House, 2008.

The question I always receive from clients and players is how to stay in the zone or create these shots they know they are capable of. The skill is in you already, you just need to learn how to create the state and emotion that will allow it to show up.

>>>>>YOUR NEXT STEP >>>>>

Chapter 5 - ACE Performance Training Guide Homework

Go to Chapter Five **Your Words Equal Your Beliefs** in your guide and answer the reflective questions and complete the Goal Setting & Language and VAK exercise.

If you haven't already purchased and downloaded your copy of *The ACE Performance Journal,* you can get it here:

http://golf-thelastsixinches.com

#1 Tool for Peak Performance: The Pre-Shot Routine

Let's Prepare for Greatness

"Decide, Commit, Swing."

– Vision54

THE TWO TOOLS FOR PEAK PERFORMANCE

In the next two chapters, I am going to introduce you to two very important tools for performing great shots. The Pre-Shot Routine and the Post-Shot Routine. These routines are different and happen at different times on the golf course. As you can imagine, the pre-shot occurs before you hit your shot and the post-shot routine occurs after the shot. Each had various components in them; in these chapters, we will break down each routine.

THE SUCCESS PROTOCOLS FOR PEAK PERFORMANCE

The illustration on the left explains the tools we will be using to create and sustain peak performance on the golf course. The illustration on the right also corresponds with the performance cycle. For example, the tools to use for your thought process is the Caddy Box and the tool to use for the before shot and during shot emotions and actions will be the Play Box. The tool for after shot emotions and anchors will be a post-shot routine.

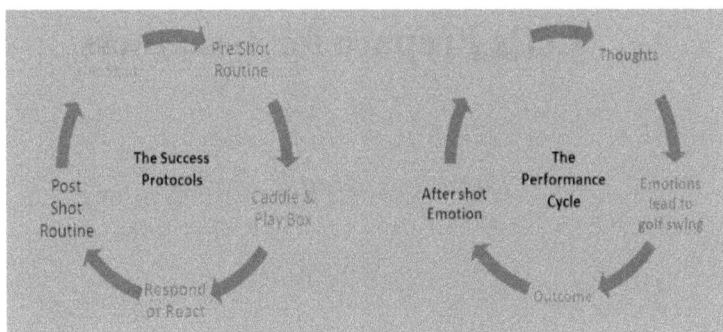

This illustration on the left is The Success Protocol showing you the tools you will be using to get what you really want on the golf course.

The illustration on the right is The Performance Cycle and is the reasons why you get what you get on the golf course.

COMPONENTS FOR EACH ROUTINE

Your success will come from **CREATING** the following:

- **A fluid, consistent pre-shot routine with:**
    - o A Caddy Box to collect data and prepare to perform
    - o A childlike Play Box

- **Post-shot routines that build confidence and trust with:**

o   Positive Anchors which will build
peak performance retention

Creating your own processes within each of these two steps is called the "Art of Playing" your Peak Performance.

PEAK PERFORMANCE TOOL #1–THE PRE-SHOT ROUTINE

The pre-shot shot routine is where you get ready to perform. The pre-shot routine has two components called the Think Box and Play box. This concept was first developed by Lynn Marriott and Pia Nilsson from Vision 54.[17] For more information on Vision 54 and Lynn Marriott and Pia Nilsson's work, check out the references in the back of this book. They call it the Think Box; I like to call it the Caddy Box because it's where you prepare to get ready to perform and achieve unlimited possibilities on the golf course.

Here is an example for LPGA Tour Professional Sandra Gal Pre Shot routine[18]:

During the first part of my routine, I gather information about the shot: the distance, the lie, the wind, the pin position. According to my game plan in combination with the way my game is going that day, as well as my feel (which apart from all the numbers is a very important ingredient in choosing the right club), I decide on a certain club and shot type. Once I decide, the most important moment during the pre-shot routine occurs: the moment I commit to my decision. This is the moment, where I transition from thinking to no-thinking. At least no conscious thinking. Unless the outside conditions change, there is no way back and I

---

[17] Nilsson, Pia, and Lynn Marriott. Every Shot Must Have a Purpose. New York: Gotham Books, 2005.

[18] "Sandra Gal diary: Perfecting a pre-shot routine - USA Today." 2015. 24 Sep. 2015

trust the first part of my routine. The better I manage to do this, the better my result.

The second part of my routine is all about staying in the present. As I mentioned, the goal is to not think, which is however, virtually impossible. So how do we get as close as we can to not thinking and being focused on where we want the ball to go?

It's actually quite easy – focus on something that keeps you in the present. This could be bunch of different things.

For example, keeping the image of the flagstick in your mind, or focusing on light grip pressure, or seeing the trajectory of the shot you envisioned or "feeling" the shot you are about to hit. There are many different ways to keep your mind focused, but all of these tools have one thing in common: they keep you focused on what you want and not on want you don't want. They keep you focused on the task at hand. You can play with it to find the right tool for you and you may also develop different alternatives.

It takes a bit of courage and commitment, but what doesn't?

Pre Shot Routine- 2 Components

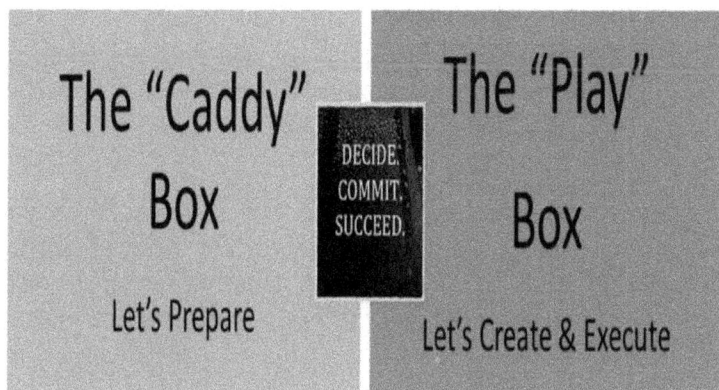

The "Caddy" Box

DECIDE, COMMIT, SUCCEED.

The "Play" Box

Let's Prepare

Let's Create & Execute

As mentioned in the Sandra Gal article, the Caddy Box is the first step in the pre-shot routine. Think about what caddies do for their players; they help to determine the shot, think about the yardage, the lies, the situation at hand, and also figure in how the player is playing that day.[19] Maybe the player doesn't have their "A" game today, so that must be figured into the preparation phase of the shot. Sometimes you may hit your six iron 160 yards, and some days you strike it 155 yards. It doesn't matter; golf is played each shot and each day. Every shot is different and every round of golf is different. Most players make the mistake of thinking they will hit the same club the same distance every round; that is not the truth. Modifications will need to be made based on many factors.

---

[19] Sandra Gal diary: Perfecting a pre-shot routine - USA Today." 2015. 24 Sep. 2015

The Caddy Box or the Think Box (as Vision 54 calls it), is where you prepare for your shot and make clear decision on your intentions. The Caddy Box is where you use the left side of your brain. Using your left brain is crucial here because your left brain specializes in the following functions:

- Logic/reason
- Thinking in words
- Remembering details in parts and very specific
- Analyzing and break apart
- Thinking sequentially

You want to collect as much data as you can so you can prepare properly. Details are important here. Focusing on specific targets is key in the Caddy Box because you don't want your focus to go to where you don't want the golf ball to end up.

The following things need to be considered while in the Caddy Box:

- What story are you beginning to tell yourself in the Caddy Box?
- What conversations are you having with your internal caddy?
- What data are you collecting from all your senses? Yardage, lie, weather, player type today, etc...
- What type of decision are you making based on your desires and wants? These decisions should come from the data collected coming from the target.
- Decide what you want to do with the shot based on data collection.

The Caddy Box is commitment time and decision time. You must make a clear decision on what club you are going to hit the golf ball with and step into the Play Box. The Caddy

Box has three parts. They are the State, Story, and Strategy.

THE CADDY BOX STATE

Creating a peak performance state of mind and a physical readiness state in the Caddy Box is crucial to hitting great golf shots. Before you go up to your shot, you will need to be aware of how you feel and what you are thinking about. This is what we call creating a state to allow peak performance to show up.

Before hitting your shot, you should feel confident and committed, not fearful and undecided. When you are in the Caddy Box, you want to be empowered.

- Are there times when, on the golf course, you were walking up to or standing over a shot, you just knew this next shot was going to be like the last one - not a very good one?
- Did you feel fearful about what is to come?

Thinking in the Caddy Box is where you start your golf swing. Remember, your thoughts create your emotions and your emotions create your golf swing. After collecting the shot data, what type of questions are you asking yourself? Are you committed and ready? This should be a resounding YES!

If not, you are not ready to perform. If you answered NO to that question, what story is going on in your head to cause the non-commitment to the shot?

The 2 Different States of Mind
"Trying versus Trusting"

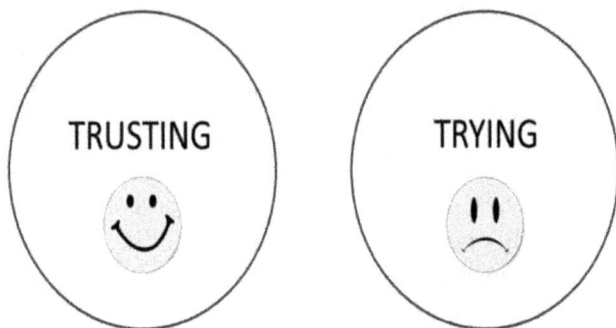

TRUSTING

TRYING

To produce great results in any sport or profession, you must trust your skills. In golf, you must take that trust into every shot with the pre-shot routine. What is the difference between trusting and trying?

The word TRYING can have a very negative meaning. When used as an adjective, it can describe – annoyance, frustration, difficulty; all the wrong images for good performance. The biggest adverse effect it is going to have on our golf swings is through physical tension. If a golfer feels physical tension, his rhythm and balance will be affected.

Trying makes the physical body feel like it has to produce something or make manipulations in the golf swing. A fluid golf swing does not come from a trying state of mind. Trying to do something with your golf swing is not peak performance language to the body. Balance, rhythm, and physical relaxation are all interrelated to an efficient golf swing. When a golfer tries to swing or tries to hit a certain club shorter or further on the golf course, these two crucial components will be affected.

Trying usually means you are trying to control something you can't control, such as your downswing.

Remember, the golf swing is a dynamic motion, not something you can pick apart while in motion. A trying state of mind has non-peak performance written all over it. Trying creates self-doubt, and the harder you try at making a change, the worse the results. The more you stay in the trying mindset, the more frustrated you will become. The harder you try, the more your skills and performance level decline.

The trying mindset means you don't trust yourself, and you are usually trying to control things that are out of your control. As you lose more control, frustration increases and mistrust builds within you. Trying creates a mindset of looking for answers outside of your own skill sets. This is not a good place to be while playing in competitions or working on achieving your best scores on the golf course.

THE TRUST MINDSET

A trust mindset, however, will help you find your peak performance zone and maintain it. Trusting allows your skills set to show up on the golf course. Trusting keeps your brain balanced in an alpha state. An alpha state is a condition of relaxed, peaceful wakefulness which gives the person feelings of tranquility and a lack of tension and anxiety.

A trust state of mind will give you certainty. Trust gives you the conviction that you have the skills set to perform the shot you want to perform. Trust is also a mindset that keeps you clear on what you can control on the golf course and accepting what you can't control. A trust mindset gives you the ability to believe in yourself and not things outside of yourself.

Creating a trusting mindset in your pre-shot routine is crucial to great shots. I teach my players to be very aware of what mindset they are in when stepping into the Play Box.

YOUR LANGUAGE IS YOUR REALITY

Your language is your belief and your self-talk comes from your beliefs. If you have beliefs that limit your potential, then you will likely accept limited results in your golf and in your life. What and how we say things to others and to ourselves is a direct result of our thought processes based on our beliefs. That's why it is important to acknowledge the role of language in our lives. We are constantly engaged with language. We describe, narrate, and judge all that happens around us. The way we speak is a very accurate reflection of how we think.[20]

Language usage is very strong determining factor in our mind set. Just meaning of words can create a shift in emotions. For example, you say to yourself, *"I am going to try and make this putt."* Is that statement a positive belief or a negative belief? In other words, is the statement empowering or disempowering?

What does the word "TRY" really mean. To me, it is a noncommittal word and creates a mindset of disbelief. The word, and action, of TRY is limiting. Either you think you will make this putt or you don't think you will. Which is it?

Let's just change the same statement to *"I AM going to make this putt."* Is this statement an empowering or disempowering belief? The difference between I "WANT TO" or going to "TRY" and "I AM" shifts the subconscious to believing you have a chance at making this putt.

Let's look at another example. Just think about what you say to yourself when you are hitting shots. Do you use the word TRY? I would bet you use it more than you think you use it. You really are not engaged in the activity if you are trying. Trusting in yourself is a different engagement both emotionally and physically. You are fully engaged, and the body will feel different when you trust yourself on the golf course.

How many times do you hear yourself say, *"Well, I am not sure about this shot, so I will **try** a six iron."*? How would that statement make your body feel when striking the golf ball?

---

[20] "Thoughts - Mind-Sets." MindSets. Accessed October 7, 2015.

Empowered and committed or fearful and tentative?

Let's change the statement to a more empowering one. *"I am sure this is my six iron. It's the perfect club for this distance."*

Now, you step up and strike the shot. How does your body feel when you are sure of what you want and where you are going?

Have you ever been on the golf course and just felt the shot was going to be good, like a putt on green or a shot off the fairway? How did you create that shot?

Have you ever been on the golf course and you just knew the shot was not going to be good and you struck the ball anyway? What was the result?

Remember golf is like life and life is like golf. Trusting is a much better feeling with yourself than trying.

CREATING DESIRABLE OUTCOMES AND GREAT SHOTS

Once you learn how to create trusting feelings in your pre-shot routine, you will need to train those feelings both on the range and on the golf course. Training your trust does not come from the hitting of golf balls with the same club over and over again. Trust comes from training yourself to strike one golf shot at time to an intended target just like on the golf course.

Golf is the only sport we don't practice on the playing field, and I think that is why people do not get better. The formula of going to the range and hitting golf balls for hours with same few clubs is the definition of insanity. You know that definition of doing the same thing over and over again and expecting different results? That formula of being a "scrape and hit" golfer of balls on the range doesn't create peak performance. I learned the game on the golf course because we didn't have practice ranges back in my hometown. I had to learn the game on the practice field called the golf course. It made me a much better player, much faster.

Today, most cities have some type of a range, whether indoor or outdoor, where you can go practice. What you want to do is practice your pre-shot routine, create a trustworthy state of mind within yourself one shot at a time, even one club at a time. The pre-shot routine will help you develop confidence.

PRACTICE LIKE YOU PLAY TRAINING DRILL

A great PLAY training drill on the range is to play 18 holes in your mind while creating one shot at a time, just like you are on the golf course. You probably have a golf course you play often and can visualize every hole. After you warm up, the purpose of the drill is to start with the club you would hit off the first tee, then go through your pre-shot routine and pick a target on the range. Give yourself the boundaries of the fairway, just like on the that first hole in your mind.

After striking the tee shot, hit the next shot with the club you think you would need as if you are on the golf course. If you landed in the fairway, then hit your fairway wood, or hybrid, or long iron (whichever club that might be depending on how the driver went). If you missed the fairway, then place the ball in a not-so-good lie on the range and practice your pre-shot routine here as well. Execute the shot as if you were paying it on the golf course (same conditions, lie yardages, club, etc.). Even go the putting green after you have hit your approach shot to your imaginary green.

The goal is to hit every shot one ball at a time with different clubs and practice your pre-shot routine. See how many holes you can play on the range before you start losing focus or start thinking about the mechanics of your golf swing.

THE CADDY BOX STORY

The story in your head should not be about the what if's or I am afraid of doing this. The story in your head should be telling you what you want to do, not what you don't want to do or what you are fearful of. The story in your head should be, *"This is what I want to do and now I trust myself to do it."*

You must have a vision of seeing yourself being successful and performing the shot you desire. If your story is creating a fearful vision or a negative result, we need to change that channel in your head.

Be aware of what state you are in once you cross over the commitment line. If you are not in the ready-set-go, state of mind, then you need to back out of the Play Box and start the routine over. You must completely trust yourself when you're in the Play Box.

THE CADDY BOX STRATEGY

What strategy are you using to create that readiness state of mind and body? Can you be your own best friend in the Caddy Box or do you have to have a method to remind yourself to create your state of readiness and confidence? The Act As If... strategy is a great way to change the story; you practice seeing yourself hit great shots in your mind. You don't have to be on the golf course to practice this. You can practice it anywhere you choose. Paying attention to what story and visions you have in your head is the first step of changing that story.

Your emotional and physical state will change your story and your story will change your emotional state. After hitting a good shot, feeling great about yourself and telling yourself, *"That was a great shot, Sue,"* helps your body feel better. When you feel better, you walk differently. Think about it. When you feel good, how do you walk? Shoulders slumped with your head down? No, you walk upright and proud with your head held high. Well, you can walk upright with head held high even before you hit your shots. You can use this strategy to help you get ready for your shots.

Walking up to the next shot with confidence helps start your pre-shot routine on a good note; your body language and the story in your head is positive. You create the thought and the emotion you want. This strategy kicks off a great pre-shot routine because it keeps you in the present moment and you don't think about the last shot.

This is why caddies on tour get paid handsomely; they keep their players calm and focused on the right mentality while on the golf course. Caddies help them with shot selection and club selections, but many times if you listen to golf on television, you can hear the caddies say to their players, "You've got this. This is your shot. This is your perfect distance or perfect club." You can do the same for yourself, you just need to practice being in the peak performance mindset, learn positive self-talk, and practice these methods on the range and on the golf course one shot at a time.

THE PLAY BOX - IT'S SHOW TIME!

The Play Box is where the right side of your brain kicks in. The right side of your brain is where the imagination is stored. It's the creative side of the brain. The right side of your brain has the following functions:

- Uses intuition and emotions
- Thinks in pictures
- Deals with whole pieces and relationships
- Will synthesize and put together facts
- Thinks holistically

You may have heard of right brainers who are plastic surgeons for their creativity to restore a burned victim with a beautiful new face, artists who created a piece of art, or musicians who can play masterful pieces of music. These are right brain dominant people.

Peak performance comes when you use both sides of your brain. Some people are dominant left brain and some people are right brain dominant. It doesn't matter which you are; however, it does matter which side of the brain you are using in the success protocol of pre-shot and post-shot routines.

If you are a right brainer, then you want to work on using you left brain when picking out targets. Maybe you don't pay attention to details of the greens when hitting shots. Remember, right brains don't pay attention to details. That is why having a left-brain caddy would be a great combination for the right brain person, and the same is true for left brain person. The left-brain person tends to be overly analytical in the Play Box and they don't know how to activate the creative side of the right brain. You will need to practice to be free and creative in the Play Box. You must train yourself, if you are left brainer, that the Play Box is just that, time to PLAY, not think.

HOW TO PRACTICE IF YOU ARE A RIGHT OR LEFT BRAINER

In *Dark Night, Early Dawn*, Christopher Bache describes the brain in this way, "When the brain hemispheres are working together, a number of known benefits result, including heightened awareness, improved recall, more self-programming flexibility and heightened creativity." Practicing playing golf would be more beneficial to a left-brain person not practicing their swing, and the opposite is true for right brain people because they tend just want to go play and not practice the details. Both golfers have strengths and weaknesses that they must work on to create a whole brain integration in their golf swing. That is what the success protocol is all about. It is a process, and each piece of the protocol must be trained. Just like you train a new golf swing or a new putting stroke, you work on parts of it until you have mastered it, then you move on. Same is true with pre-shot and post-shot routines.

The Play Box has two parts: State and Strategy.

THE PLAY BOX STATE

- What state of mind are you in and how does your body feel while in the Play Box?
- Are you thinking positive as you walk into the play box?
- Are you feeling empowered in your Play box?
- Do you trust your decision on how you going to play the shot?

If not, you don't belong in there. Many times, players think they are thinking positively consciously; however, when they step into the Play Box, something happens in their mind and subconsciously self-sabotaging thoughts occur. Due to these thoughts, the shot doesn't come out as consciously intended. At times, players are aware this is happening, and sometimes they are not aware of their senses during the play box. It's important that players become mindful of their thoughts and feelings in the Play Box.

You must be clear with your intentions, have trust in yourself, and feel great. How does your body feel in the Play Box? Athletic or stiff and tense? As Lynn Marriott from Vision54 states, "Be an athlete in the Play Box."[21]

You must be ready to move freely and easily. Athletes don't think about how to move, they just move. Allow your training to free your body up and allow it to create shots you set your intentions on.

THE PLAY BOX STRATEGY

Remember, a strategy means you must put something into action to achieve your overall objective.

What strategy are you using to get into an empowering state of mind so that your true authentic golf swing comes out to produce what you want?

---

[21] Nilsson, Pia, and Lynn Marriott. Every Shot Must Have a Purpose. New York: Gotham Books, 2005.

Sports psychologists used to think everyone, in order to perform at high levels, needed to be in high arousal mode; however, research tells us each player is different. Arousal states need to match the individual personality and makeup of the player. Some athletes need to have a high state of arousal to get ready to perform. What level do you need to be able to create great shots?

You can see different personalities on the golf course. Some players play slower than others, some players play faster than others. Some players are more emotional after great shots, some are not. What works for you? In the next couple of paragraphs, we will introduce you to a few examples of Play box strategies.

HUMMING

The first great Play box strategy is humming. Yes, humming in the Play Box keeps your brain busy and free from distractions. Your brain can't hum and give your mind mechanical thought or direction. Humming creates a playful, childlike mind. A childlike mind will create a free-flowing feeling of trust and allow you to execute good shots. Try it, you will be amazed on how humming quiets the mind.

FOCUS ON TARGET, TARGET, TARGET

The next Play box strategy is called target focused. Some players completely focus their language and their eyes on the target. They have a dialogue with the target. They visualize the target and the shot they want to play. For example, Jason Day, PGA Tour Professional, right before he steps into the Play Box sees his target, closes his eyes, and visualizes the shot as if he is playing it in his mind. He visualizes what he wants to do as if he sees himself hitting the shot. You can use this strategy both in the Caddy Box and Play Box.

THE STEP OUT STRATEGY

Another Play box strategy is called the Step out. If you are not feeling empowered, ready, and engaged with the target, you MUST step out of the box and reload the pre-shot routine. I guarantee that if you don't step out of the Play Box, you will not like the result. Think of it like a pitcher and a batter in a baseball game. The pitcher is getting ready to pitch and the batter steps into her batter's box, now the pitcher isn't quite ready and starts to read signals from the catcher; it's taking longer than the batter likes, so the batter steps out. The batter is controlling the situation and doesn't stay in the batter's box until they are completely ready to receive the pitch. This cat and mouse game is played with our minds many times on the golf course, as well as when we are preparing for the shot. However, at times, we don't step out of the box and we swing and miss the shot just like the batter swings and misses the pitch.

If you are not ready and committed to the shot, step out of the Play Box. It only takes a minute to reload and rehearse your pre-shot routine again. Reloading your pre-shot routine will take less time that looking for the errant shot you hit because you didn't step out of the Play Box due to fear or anxiety for not being fully committed to the shot.

Whatever strategy you use, you want it to match your intentions of producing great results. This is why we teach players to pay attention to when they are playing well, what are they doing, thinking, saying, responding, etc. Remember, mechanical thoughts do not belong in the Play Box.

You have already collected all the details you need in the Caddy Box. This is where most golfers stumble. They take their mechanical thoughts and the "how to swing" thoughts into the Play Box; big mistake.

When you drive your car, you do not think about all the muscle movements you need to press the gas pedal or press on the brake and at the same time think about which hand is steering the wheel and which hand is turning a wheel.

The Play Box is where we want the subconscious to take

over. We want to be creative, open, curious to what is out in front of us with no expectations.

WHAT YOU RESIST, WILL PERSIST

If you are afraid of hooking a shot off the tee, guess what happens? You either hook it because that is your focus, and you mind controls the body and the body controls the golf swing. Another scenario, you make sure you don't hook it and manipulate the golf swing to be sure it doesn't hook, and you end up overcompensating and the ball slices out of bounds. This occurs because of your thoughts are not on your golf swing. Again, not good pre-shot routine state of mind.

If you have expectations or focus on mechanics, your true authentic swing will not show up and your outcomes will not be satisfactory. We can have an intention for the golf shot that comes from stepping up to the ball with a purpose in mind; however, during the swing while in the Play Box, we must stay creative and open to create the shot we intended to imagine in our minds. Our goal in the Play Box is to Create and Execute shots.

>>>>>Next Step>>>>>

Chapter 6 - ACE Performance Training Guide Homework

Go to Chapter Six **#1 Tool for Peak Performance: The Pre-Shot Routine** in your guide and answer the reflective questions and complete the Create a State and Brain Dominance exercises.

If you haven't already purchased and downloaded a copy of
The ACE Performance Training Guide,
you can get it here:

http://golf-thelastsixinches.com

#2 Tool for Peak Performance: The Post-Shot Routine

"There is no failure, only feedback."

– Robert Allen

THE POST-SHOT ROUTINE

The post-shot routine is what you say to yourself after the shot. It's how you feel after the shot. It's what you do after a shot. Unfortunately, when you watch golf on television, most of the time the broadcast doesn't show players post-shot routine, yet it is one of the most important parts of the success protocol for peak performance.

Why is the post-shot routine so important? Your post-shot routine is where you:

- Assess to learn about our game
- Evaluate for our next opportunity
- Learn the Emotional Neutral Response
- Evaluate from factual perspective
- Respond instead of react

You want to store good shots in your long-term memory

and learn to create emotionally neutral responses to the bad shots. Your body is a marvelous sensory machine and what you emotionalize, you remember. When you smell a food that you grew up with, your brain takes you back to the memory. That is what is called a long-term memory. Remember, our long-term memory is stored in the subconscious. When we have a high level of emotion, our cells fire in our nervous system and we make more cells that store that emotion. It's described as "cells that fire together, wire together."[22] This is part of the new neuroscience research telling us that our brains can be modified.

THE PURPOSE OF THE POST-SHOT ROUTINE

The post-shot routine is where we, as golfers, can really assess each part of our game. You can use a notebook or software to track your shots, but you also want to track your emotional responses to shots. Being mindful of shots and results can be very beneficial to golfers who are looking to find ways to build confidence and continually grow as players.

While many golfers know about, and use, pre-shot routines, most forget the necessity of a post-shot routine, especially after a bad shot. They are left open to several problems that can damage their overall play.

After a bad shot or putt, many of us would lose focus, tense up, and waste energy on disempowering thoughts and actions. These disempowering actions and behaviors after bad shots do nothing but interfere with the next shot. All of this can be avoided by being prepared with a solid post-shot routine. The post-shot routine has three parts: State, Story, and Strategy

THE POST-SHOT STATE

---

[22] "Timing is everything: scientists control rapid rewiring of ..." 2014. 6 Sep. 2015 <https://www.mcgill.ca/channels/news/timing-everything-scientists-control-rapid-re-wiring-brain-circuits-using-patterned-visual-stimulati-236849>

Your state of mind and the state of your body are really important during a post-shot routine. Remember, what we tend to highly emotionalize, our body will store that memory. It is crucial to be mindful what state of mind we are in after good shots and bad shots. With good shots, good players own the shot, feel good about themselves, and build confidence. With bad shots, players emotionalize and often create feelings of mistrust and fear. Confidence building does not come from feelings of fear and lack of trust on the golf course.

YOUR EMOTIONS

When you make a bad shot, emotions are going to come out. That is very normal for human beings; however, it's how you deal with those emotions that is important. Everyone has good and bad days on the golf course, but peak performers know that if their day is not going well, they deal with their emotions differently than non-peak performers. There will be days you will feel disappointed, frustrated, or even angry at times. The key is to use strategies to neutralize those emotions.

Your emotions can create your state of mind. How so? When you have emotions, you get into the cycle of thoughts become emotions, emotions become actions. The key, again, is to be mindful of where your emotions and thoughts are taking you. Do your emotions and thoughts create a state of empowerment?

It's easy to change your state because you have control of your thoughts and your actions. The key is to understand that emotions and thoughts are going to come and go. You need to develop the tools and strategies to help you respond to them appropriately so they don't affect your performance.

If you are not managing your emotions, they are managing you. Recognize which emotions keep you in the zone or the ones that keep you from your zone.

THE STORY IN YOUR HEAD

After hitting a shot, what story or narrative comes to mind? That will probably depend on what type of shot you hit. The key about the post-shot routine is not to let the story in your head go negative or disempower you. Remember, you have control of your thoughts and emotions. Be aware of what story begins in your mind after good shots. Do you disown them, just ignore them, or call them lucky? Do you own your good shots and take credit for them? This will build your self-confidence.

After hitting bad shots, where does the story in your head go? Do you give the bad shots more focus than the good shots? What narrative starts to build in your mind after the bad shot? Can you let it go?

The old saying is if you're in your head, you're dead. If you let the story in your head dictate the state of mind you are in, then the story is empowering you. You better be careful where the story in your mind is going.

Is the story in your head making you feel positive or negative, empowered or disempowered? This is where self-talk can help if the story is going negative. If you're mindful, you can re-direct your thoughts with self-talk. I call it talking yourself into the peak performance state of mind. This will build confidence versus talking yourself out of the peak performance state of mind.

An example of this was when one of my clients came to me stating he could not play consistently. One shot would be fine then the next shot ended up horribly. I went out on the golf course and watched him play for nine holes. I just watched his behavior before and after shots, during good and bad shots. He never acknowledged his good shots, but when he hit the bad shots, he owned them by giving them attention. His self-talk was, *"You stupid idiot, why did you do that?"* His anchoring of bad shots was numerous, while the anchoring of good shots was minimal.

His post-shot routine of anchoring only the bad shots was creating more bad shots. His story in his head was, *"I am not consistent; therefore, I am going to hit more bad shots."* He gave all his energy to bad shots, and his outcome was more bad shots. The story in his head was telling him that he was not a consistent player; therefore, that is what he received. His mind only gave focus to the bad shots without giving much credit to any of his good shots. Remember, your story comes from your beliefs and your beliefs come from your past and what you anchor and give energy to through your emotions and your thoughts.

LANGUAGING, FOCUS, AND PHYSIOLOGY

Tony Robbins tells us that our mindset, or state of mind, will change our story in our head and also change the strategies we use to solve problems.[23] If you want to create a change, you must pay attention to your mindset and state of being while you play golf.

Imagine you are driving to the golf course, and you don't feel 100% that day. What type of narrative or story begins to play in your mind? Do thoughts show up like, *"Well, I am not going to play well today and I am just not feeling very well,"* or *"Oh, I am playing with so and so and she /he is very competitive, and I don't feel like being competitive today."* Think about what type of stories go on in your head when you start to drive to the golf course.

We can create a state and we can change our state in a second if we wish and know how. We can change our language and our self-talk immediately if we recognize our self-talk and reframe into a positive language. Say to yourself, *"I don't feel well today; however, I am going to enjoy myself no matter what because I am playing with my best friend whom I have not seen in awhile."* Going back to gratefulness and engaging on the real reason you are playing, your story in your head will change,

---

[23] Robbins, Anthony. Awaken the Giant Within: How to Take Immediate Control of Your Mental, Emotional, Physical & Financial Destiny! New York: Free Press, 2003

changing your state.

If you are not feeling so well that day, can you change your physiology? Of course you can! People say you can fake it until you make it, and that is true. Could you stand taller, prouder, and act like you feel great and just accept who you are that day? Your body will feel differently every day, so how will you manage that? You manage it by managing your state of mind and attitude about it.

RESPONDING VERSUS REACTING IN POST-SHOT ROUTINES

In post-shot routines, it is very important to learn how to respond to shots, not react. Why? People think responding and reacting are the same behavior, but that is not true. Responding is more empowering behavior and reacting is disempowering. Responding gives you opportunity to see the big picture in the situation; therefore, it gives you better problem-solving skills and more productive thinking. Responding allows you to collect data and focus on the facts.

You intend to hit a fairway off the first tee, you go through your normal pre-shot routine and strike the ball. The ball doesn't go where you intended it to go. It ends up in the left deep rough. You have a choice, you can react or respond. If you respond, you might say to yourself, *"Well, that was not like me,"* and not emotionalize it. Keeping the emotions to neutral will allow time for your brain to start collecting the data and facts. Such statements like, *"Well, it's in the rough. It's not the end of the world, and I can find that golf ball."*

Let's look at some synonyms for the word reacting from the Webster Dictionary. Reacting means we actually need to do something:

- answer back
- backfire
- boomerang
- echo

- reciprocate
- get back at
- give a snappy comeback
- talk back

Reacting is disempowering. Reacting is unproductive.

Reacting causes us to jump to conclusions, and we end up seeing the short sightedness of the situation. We then lose the opportunity to see the big picture. Continuous reacting to situations on the golf course causes us to learn how to overreact. Overreacting will emotionally energize the memory that we really want to forget. However, by emotionalizing it with so much energy, we are actually doing the opposite. We are storing it only for it to reappear in the future. After we hit a golf shot, we don't need to do anything except learn from it. We can't bring the shot or experience back, it is gone. That is the good news about golf. You get to let it go and move on. However, if you learn to react, then you are not letting that not so good shot go. You are storing it, and it will return again someday, sometime in your golfing life. It may be showing up all the time and now you can see why.

Imagine you have a hole on your golf course that you do not like playing because you have bad memories. You seem to play poorly on the hole every time you play. Think about why you perform that way. You probably start to bring the memory of all those not so great experiences to your tee shot, and before you have even stuck the golf ball, you have sabotaged yourself. You get what you think about. You need to change your thoughts and change your state of mind and attitude about the hole. Even if you have never had a good experience on that hole before, you need to come up with a different memory or thought before you start you pre-shot routine.

This is where I teach our players to go to their happy place. Your happy place is where you feel secure, loved and grateful. The happy place exercise creates a state of well-being.

Your mind doesn't know the difference between good and bad until you bring attention to the bad experience. It's the same as the self-fulfilling prophecy theory. You get what you ask for. Golf shots are not meant to be judged. Golf shots give us an opportunity to learn something about ourselves as a person, as a human being. The human being directs the golf swing, not the other way around. However, we find that is not the case with most golfers; they let their golf swing determine who they are. Even not so good shots should be feedback, not failure. You can learn something from every shot, no matter the outcome if you train yourself to think that way.

The post-shot routine is all about feedback, not failure. If you hit a not so good shot and you think you failed, then what state of mind will that put you in? Positive or negative? Your thoughts, emotions, and actions start to change to the cycle of non-peak performance. Thoughts start coming to mind like, *"What's wrong with me? I need to fix something. I failed."* Failure is defined as the lack of success, decay, falling short. Just think about the meaning behind those words. What kind of state would those words put you in?

ANCHORING SHOTS

You want to teach yourself to anchor the good and forget the not-so-good. What you do or say after a shot is also what I call an anchor. Where you put your energy and focus, those shots and emotions will re-appear. By getting upset and uptight over the bad shots and replaying them over and over in your mind, you are really rehearsing for more troubles.

Remember, you will anchor and store these memories because it becomes emotionally charged in your nervous system.

In the post-shot routine, I teach my players that they must pay attention to what they anchor. An anchor, as a verb, is defined as the means to cause to be firmly attached; "fasten onto and lock in." As a noun, an anchor is defined as something that grounds a ship and keeps it from moving. How ironic that an anchor will prevent you from moving anywhere. This is a perfect metaphor for golf.

What strategies are you using to anchor the good shot in your rounds? Maybe you don't even realize you are anchoring any shots.

What are you locking in, the positive or the negative thoughts, emotions and actions? What are you saying to yourself after striking the ball when you play? If you hit a good shot do you say, *"Nice shot!"* or, *"Well, that was lucky."* When you hit a bad shot, what do you say to yourself? *"Oh well, that was not like me,"* or, *"Well, that was stupid of me."* Which statement has more energy to it?

These statements cause emotions to fire up in our nervous system. If we emotionalize with high energy, we will anchor that memory and feeling in our long-term memory causing us to remember it for future use. Remember that phrase, *for future use.*

I had a client who, after shots, would emotionalize only the not so good shots. She would hit a shot that didn't turn out well, and she would say things like, *"You stupid idiot! What are you doing? You can't play worth a darn."* This language at times would get more intense. She would emotionalize the bad shots and this in turn anchors the memory into her long-term memory. When she hit good shots, she did not really pay attention or give herself credit. She was actually emotionally neutralizing the good shots and emotionally intensifying the not so good shots. The nervous system and the brain love to store memories that we intensify. This was the reason she was always getting more not so good shots. If you want more good shots, you must emotionalize them and pay more attention to you when you hit good shots.

Building confidence in your post shot routine is crucial to moving into the next shot with a peak performance mindset. Anchoring positive emotions and images into your long-term memory will set you up for a much better chance of hitting a good shot. If you anchor the negative emotions and the bad shots, you are building up more negative experiences. That will show up again on the golf course as well. Be careful what emotions you are anchoring. You want your post shot routines to help you close the last shot and move onto the next shot with clarity and confidence. Anchoring positive emotions and experiences will help you develop ways to create your peak performances on the golf course.

I tell my students to use their successes as building blocks. You must congratulate yourself after a good shot. You must learn how to own the good shots. Give yourself a verbal or physical cue to end the visualization. For example, say "Good Shot, Sue!" Adding your name allows your brain to own that shot. Adding your name to that statement also makes it more meaningful to you; you made the shot, why not own it?

Some players like to make a physical move to anchor the positive feeling. Making a physical move like a fist pump or high five anchors the good feeling from the shot, wires the feeling into the nervous system, and anchors it into long term memory. Remember, what you give energy to will anchor into your mind and body creating memories, so be careful what you want to own and anchor. The idea is to reward your efforts so that your mind strives to reproduce that feeling on each subsequent shot. We want long term memories of good shots not long-term memories of bad shots.

Never, ever walk away from a shot until you have created a positive mental image or positive feeling moving forward. This is what we call closing the shot. We learned something from the bad shot and we anchored the good shot. It is that simple. After letting go and closing the last shot, you are now free to create a brand new shot. Rinse and Repeat.

Dropping strokes in your golf game will occur if your post shot routines lead you to positive images. Finding your zone, or peak performance, will happen if you follow a positive anchor or an emotionally neutral response.

OTHER POST-SHOT STRATEGIES

The Breath

When under pressure or when you are hitting bad shots, your emotions are going to try and get the best of you. It is up to you to be mindful of this. Learning to properly breathe will keep your emotions evenly balanced. Poor breathing increases anxiety, so practice breathing right. Deep breathing means you must learn how to produce a deep cleansing breath. Breathing properly will allow the body to calm down and relax faster on the golf course. To breathe properly you must inhale and allow the oxygen to fill up the belly, not the chest. Stressful breathing is breathing from the chest.

Unconscious breathing is not easy or smooth. Most people's breath tends to be tense, shallow and erratic, and occur within the chest cavity, not the diaphragm.

We became used to breathing from our chest, using only a fraction of the lungs, not knowing that this unhealthy and unnatural way of inhaling may lead to several complications. With proper breathing, called yoga or pranayama breathing, we increase the capacity of our lungs, bringing more oxygen supply to the body to function well. We learn how to breathe slowly and deeply - the right way.[24]

Benefits to Proper Breathing

- Develops our concentration and focus. It fights away stress and relaxes the body. Controlling one's breathing also results in serenity and peace of mind, which is very helpful in competitions or stressful situations on the golf course.

---

[24] "Pranayama." Gratitude Yoga. Accessed October 7, 2015.

- Proper breathing offers a better self-control. Through concentration, one can better handle temper and reactions. Mind can function clearly, avoiding arguments and wrong decisions. Moreover, self-control also involves control over one's physical body.
- Proper breathing leads to a relaxed body and mind.

Think about this when you hit a bad shot or you receive a negative outcome on the golf course, we often gasp—inhaling and then holding the breath. These breathing patterns can activate the sympathetic nervous system (often referred to as the "fight or flight response").

Proper breathing fosters a long, smooth exhale. It will support the parasympathetic nervous system and activate what is commonly known as the "relaxation response," reducing stress and its effects on your body and mind. As a result your mind becomes more focused and still, and you increase resilience on the golf course.[25] A deep cleansing breath will activate the relaxation response. You can use this breathing strategy in everyday life to calm your nerves and cope with challenges of the day.

The "Do over Shot" Image

The "Do Over Shot" Image is a strategy to use during your post-shot routine. After hitting a bad shot, take a second and think about the last shot you just hit. Here we are not going to emotionalize it, we are just going to look at the facts about the result. Again, just learn from the shot and give yourself some feedback, not negative self-talk that will create a feeling of failure. This is the difference between responding and reacting. Reacting usually emotionalizes the last bad shot. Responding to the last shot helps us neutralize and gain facts about the shot.

---

[25] "Yoga & Breathing | Try Pranayama for Stress, Anxiety, and Insomnia." Yoga Journal. June 15, 2012. Accessed October 7, 2015.

Think about what can you learn from your last shot. What types of shots do you see yourself hitting next time you are in this situation? How will you see the shot differently next time?

Secure that image in your mind before walking away from the last shot. See yourself being successful and having great results. After the rehearsal of the replacement shot, notice how that makes you feel and notice the difference. Focus on the emotions of a good shot.

Your attention must be about what's out in front of you, not what's behind you. This technique of replacement swing or routines will allow your attention to be clear and your focus will now be on the next shot. We want to be present for each and every shot. This is the hardest step and must be accomplished completely. The past is gone, and the future is not here yet, so our focus is about moving forward into the next shot.

This routine will enable you to let go of the bad shots and move forward so you can play in the present moment, not playing in the past, nor playing in the future. Practice this technique even on the range so you train yourself to perform this post-shot routine regularly on the golf course. You will be able to move from one shot to the next with ease.

NEUTRALIZING STRATEGIES FOR ANCHORING BAD SHOTS

- After the not so good shot, just wave it goodbye and say out loud, "Well, that is not like me," and move on. You must practice this verbal statement and physically wave the shot goodbye. It sounds silly I know, but your action of waving will anchor in the feeling of not owning that not so good shot. It will help you close the shot in your mind so you can move to the next shot with clear thoughts. Notice how it makes you feel. You must train yourself to be okay with letting it go. A peak performance post-shot routine would be actions and mindfulness for gaining feedback from the shot.

- Look at the shot as if you are spectator of the game, not the participant. When we act as the participant, we tend to not to own the bad shots and emotionalize them. Change the story in your head and be the spectator just watching and respond with facts, not reactions or charged emotions.

>>>>>Next Step >>>>>

Chapter 7 - ACE Performance Training Guide Homework

Go to Chapter Seven **#2 Tool for Peak Performance: The Post-Shot Routine** in your guide and answer the reflective questions and complete the Happy Place and Internal Scorecard exercises.

If you haven't already purchased a copy of
The ACE Performance Journal,
you can get it here:

http://golf-thelastsixinches.com

Conclusion

In the first chapter, you learned about knowing WHY you play this great game called golf. Knowing your real WHY well is a mindful exercise itself. Knowing why you play will help keep you motivated to play the game. It's very simple. If your goal for playing golf is to be outdoors, enjoy the nature. If you stay engaged with that one goal, then your day will be a great one. If you lose your WHY and start to play for other people or other reasons, then you are not going to have a great experience. You can create a shift immediately if you can recognize what you're doing in the present moment.

In the second chapter, you learned how thoughts, emotions, and actions dictate your golf game. Being mindful is paying attention to those thoughts, emotions, and actions. Pay attention to when you're feeling happy or not so happy and why. What are you thinking in over shots versus after-shots?

In the third chapter, you learned the powerful tool of Mindfulness and Journaling. Awareness is the first step to changing a thought or behavior, and journaling is the best way to become mindful. Hopefully, you were successful with each and completed the homework assignments in *The ACE Performance Journal.*

In the fourth chapter, you learned to focus. Focus is getting clear about what you want, whether it be your putting or your long game. If you are mindful of what you are focused on, then you can assess your game more efficiently. How do mindfulness and focus correlate? If you are mindful, you will have better ability to concentrate on what you want. Being able to focus better and more efficiently is a huge benefit in golf. Being mindful to understand when you are outcome or process oriented is also a benefit.

In the fifth chapter on Belief and Self-talk, you learned the meaning of self-talk and how it can drive your state of mind and state of being on the golf course. Being mindful of your self-talk is so important because your words are your reality. Going through the exercises in *The Ace Performance Journal* is important to determine the correlation of your self-talk and your shot outcome.

In the sixth and seventh chapters, you learned about the two crucial steps to achieving peak performance: the Pre-Shot and Post-Shot routines. We discussed the difference between trust and trying in golf. If you're being mindful, you will recognize when you're in a trusting state of mind and when you're in the trying state of mind. Remember, a trusting state of mind will empower you, and trying will be a dis-empowering state of mind.

Being mindful in the pre-shot routines and paying attention to your thoughts and emotions during your post-shot routines are important in helping you understand why you get what you get on the golf course.

If we become mindful of these three concepts of focus, language and physiology within both the pre shot and post shot routines, we will create peak performance.

Hopefully, this book, *Golf - The Last Six Inches,* taught you how to think differently about your golf game. Remember, you are not your swing; however, you are your thoughts and your emotions. Change your Brain to Change your Game by allowing your mind to take you to your own greatness.

>>>>> **Last Step** >>>>>

Conclusion - ACE Performance Training Guide Homework

Go to the Conclusion section in your guide and answer the reflective questions and complete the Focus, Language, and Physiology exercise.

If you haven't already purchased *The ACE Performance Training guide,* you can get it here:
https://golf-thelastsixinches.com

RESOURCES

Here are a few resources that have inspired me. All of the fantastic programs, books, and mentors that have been mentioned or quoted in this book, *Golf - The Last Six Inches,* are listed here. I've even included some of my favorites that aren't in the book. Take some time to explore, read, or purchase these resources while continuing your golf improvement and transformation!

You can "Change your Brain and Change any Game!"

Books
- *Golf is Not a Game of Perfect* by Dr. Bob Rotella - Filled with insightful stories about golf, this delightful book will improve the game of even the most casual weekend player.

- *Awaken the Giant Within* by Tony Robbins - This provides a step-by-step program teaching the fundamental lessons of self-mastery that will enable you to discover your true purpose, take control of your life, and harness the forces that shape your destiny.

- *The Brain That Changes Itself* by Dr. Norman Doidge - Dr. Doidge has written an immensely moving, inspiring book that will permanently alter the way we look at our brains, human nature, and human potential.

- *Every Shot Must Have A Purpose* by Pia Nilsson and Lynn Marriott - Unlike any other golf book, this offers cutting-edge techniques for integrating the physical, technical, mental, emotional, and social parts of a player's game.

- *The Biology of Belief* by Dr. Bruce Lipton - Through the research of Dr. Lipton and other leading-edge scientists, stunning new discoveries have been made about the interaction between your mind and body and the processes by which cells receive information.

- *Golf: Energy in Motion - It's Not About the Ball; It's About the Possibilities* by Dr. Debbie Crews - This book is written to enlighten golfers to perform what we want, when we want it, on the golf course. It is about performance, an integral part of learning and playing this great game of golf.

- *Extraordinary Golf: The Art of Possible* by Fred Shoemaker - Shoemaker shows how extraordinary golf can be coached, learned, and practiced, with results not only in people's scores but in their sheer pleasure in the game.

- *Attainment - The 12 Elements of Elite Performance* by Larry Bassham - 95% of all winning is accomplished by only 5% of the participants. They are the Elite. Learn the 12 elements that separates the Elite from the others.

- *The Eight Traits of Champion Golfers* by Dr Deborah

Graham and Jon Stabler - Leading sports psychologist Dr. Deborah Graham and Jon Stabler identify the eight crucial personality traits that separate true champions from the rest.

- *Easier Said than Done - The Undeniable, Tour-Tested Truths You Must Know (and Apply) to Finally Play to your Potential on the Golf Course* by Dr. Rick Jensen - Embracing Dr. Jensen's 12 Truths will help you take your struggling golf game to that wonderful next level.

Websites
- Sue Wieger Golf - My website provides more information about improving your golf game and your life. Get access to more resources, programs, and workshops! http://www.suewiegergolf.com/

- The Golf State of Mind - David Mackenzie created this site to help golfers of all levels stop making the same mental mistakes over and over again and instead use my proven process for reaching their potential. http://golfstateofmind.com/

- Abraham-Hicks & Law of Attraction - This is the original source material for the current *Law of Attraction* wave that is sweeping the world, and it is the 21st century inspiration for thousands of books, films, essays and lectures that are responsible for the current paradigm shift in consciousness. http://www.abraham-hicks.com/

- The World is All Yours - Throughout this site, you will find tons of valuable information on bettering your life and the lives around you. http://www.theworld isallyours.com/

- MindSets - Additional information about how our mindset is created by our beliefs, thoughts, and actions.

http://www.mind-sets.com/html/mindset/thoughts.htm

Articles and Videos

- "Interview: 5 Things About Mindfulness and Work" - A Life of Productivity
  http://alifeofproductivity.com/
  interview-5-things-about-mindfulness-and-work/

- "5 Online Journaling Tools" - Lifehack
  http://www.lifehack.org/articles/
  technology/5-online-journaling-tools.html

- "Journal Writing: 5 Smart Reasons Why You Should Start Doing It Today" - Lifehack
  http://www. lifehack.org/articles/communication/.html

- Important Information about PSYCH-K Balance Processes - Robert Williams, Psych K
  https://www. youtube.com/watch?v=qE_GDxDvPsc

- Purcell, M. (2013). "The Health Benefits of Journaling". *Psych Central.*
  http://psychcentral.com/
  lib/the-health-benefits-of-journaling/

- Impulse and Self-Control From a Dual-Systems Perspective Wilhelm Hofmann, Department of Psychology, University of Würzburg, Röntgenring 10, 97070 Würzburg, Germany;
  e-mail: hofmannw@psychologie.uni-wuerzburg.de.

Bibliography

"Abraham-Hicks." Abraham-Hicks. Accessed October 7, 2015.

Bache, Christopher M. Dark Night, Early Dawn: Steps to a Deep Ecology of Mind. Albany, N.Y.: State University of New York Press, 2000.

Bassham, Troy. Attainment: The 12 Elements of Elite Performance.

"Disappearance of the Universe Quote for Today." KEEN: : Law of Attraction. Accessed October 7, 2015.

Doidge, Norman. The Brain That Changes Itself: Stories of Personal Triumph from the Frontiers of Brain Science. New York: Viking, 2007.

"Journal Writing: 5 Smart Reasons Why YOU Should Start Doing It TODAY." Lifehack RSS. Accessed October 7, 2015.

Lipton, Bruce H. The Biology of Belief: Unleashing the Power of Consciousness, Matter & Miracles. Carlsbad, Calif.: Hay House, 2008.

Nilsson, Pia, and Lynn Marriott. Every Shot Must Have a Purpose. New York: Gotham Books, 2005.

"Pranayama." Gratitude Yoga. Accessed October 7, 2015.

Robbins, Anthony. Awaken the Giant Within: How to Take Immediate Control of Your Mental, Emotional, Physical & Financial Destiny! New York: Free Press, 2003.

Rotella, Robert J., and Robert Cullen. Golf Is Not a Game of

Perfect. New York: Simon & Schuster, 1995.

Rotella, Dr. Robert. Putting Like a Genius. Simon & Schuster Audio, 2010.

Sandra Gal diary: Perfecting a pre-shot routine - USA Today." 2015. 24 Sep. 2015

Shoemaker, Fred, and Pete Shoemaker. Extraordinary Golf: The Art of the Possible. New York: Berkley Pub. Group, 1997.

"The Trading Wife." Tough Day – Keeping Emotions at Bay. Accessed October 7, 2015.

"Thoughts - Mind-Sets." MindSets. Accessed October 7, 2015.

"What Is Mindfulness? - Meditation." Sharecare. Accessed October 7, 2015.

"Yoga & Breathing | Try Pranayama for Stress, Anxiety, and Insomnia." Yoga Journal. June 15, 2012. Accessed October 7, 2015.

ABOUT THE AUTHOR

Sue Wieger, M.Ed., #1 Best Selling International Author, RYI 200, and Motivational Speaker is a 21year LPGA Class "A" Golf Professional and Peak Performance Coach. She owns and operates the Sue Wieger Golf Academy (SWGA), which is an international learning and performance business.

SWGA incorporates innovative Mind and Body coaching and training techniques to maximize each individual player's potential. Sue coaches and trains all levels including PGA and LPGA players. Ms. Wieger has created a mental peak performance golf program called "**Change Your Brain, Change Your Game**" and hosts 1-3 day workshops around the country.

Ms. Wieger has a Master's Degree in Educational Psychology and a Bachelor's Degree in Education. Sue is a Psychology & Honors Program Professor as well as the Director of Education for Yoga For Golfers™. Ms. Wieger is also a Certified Golf Fitness Trainer for Tathata Golf, Titleist Performance Institute, Registered Yoga Instructor (RYI 200), and PSYCH- K Facilitator. Ms. Wieger is also a Consultant and National Golf Facility Evaluator for the National Women's Golf Alliance.

Ms. Wieger was selected as the 2015 LPGA Teacher of The Year - Central Section and as well as a finalist for LPGA Teacher of the year for 2011, 2012, and 2013. Sue has consulted with many well-known golf companies such as:

The Golf Channel, Nicklaus Flick Game Improvement Golf Schools, Women on Course, Ladies Links Fore Golf, Trivita Wellness Centers, Katherine Roberts,Yoga For Golfers™, "Golf for Women" Magazine Golf Schools, Executive Women's Golf Association, – EWGA, Ladies Links Fore Golf, The

American Long Driver's Association-ALDA, and America West Golf Vacations.

Sue is a 17year breast cancer survivor and is Founding Executive Director for the "Golf Fore Life" Breast Cancer Charity program dedicated to raising funds for breast cancer research. Sue resides in Arizona and hosts SWGA programs internationally.

Contact Sue @
www.suewiegergolf.com

or

https://golf-thelastsixinches.com

480-392-6563

SUE WIEGER
GOLF ACADEMY

Sue Wieger Golf Academy (SWGA) - A Learning and Performance Institute - has been and continues to be recognized as the premier provider of golf instructional and educational programs. SWGA is the leader in unique golf programs by providing first class service that promotes enjoyment and fulfillment to all levels while operating with the highest standards of integrity and professionalism.

Award winning golf instructor Sue Wieger LPGA offers professional golf lessons focusing on the mental, physical, and spiritual aspects of the game. Students have found significant and measurable improvements in their golf games from working with Ms. Wieger.

Sue Wieger is a 21year LPGA Class "A" Golf Professional. Ms. Wieger also has a Master's in Psychology and a Bachelor's Degree in Education. Sue is a Certified Titleist Performance Institute Golf Fitness Trainer and Yoga For Golfers Certified Instructor. Sue is also a Psychology Professor and a published golf writer who has been a featured guest on various golf shows.

Ms. Wieger creates a custom program for each student based on their unique abilities and situation. Her unique teaching methodology includes Yoga and Psychology, in addition to traditional mechanical coaching methods, to bring out the best possible performance from her students. Students frequently comment that working with Sue not only significantly improves their performance on the golf course, but also in their work and their life.

SWGA delivers learning and performance experiences that focus on effective strategies to further educate the individual's learning of golf as well as balance and happiness in life. SWGA golf programs are a medium to teach learning and performance skills that can easily be transferred into everyday life.

Contact Sue at www.suewiegergolf.com or
https://golf-the lastsixinches.com
480-392-6563